A Guide to Preaching and Leading Worship

A Guide to Preaching and Leading Worship

William H. Willimon

Westminster John Knox Press
LOUISVILLE • LONDON

Previously published as *Preaching and Leading Worship* (Philadelphia: Westminster Press, 1984).

Book design by Drew Stevens
Cover design by Night & Day Design

First edition
Published by Westminster John Knox Press
Louisville, Kentucky

This book is printed on acid-free paper that meets the American National Standards Institute Z39.48 standard. ∞

PRINTED IN THE UNITED STATES OF AMERICA

08 09 10 11 12 13 14 15 16 17 — 10 9 8 7 6 5 4 3 2 1

Library of Congress Cataloging-in-Publication Data

Willimon, William H.
  A guide to preaching and leading worship / William H. Willimon.—1st. ed.
     p. cm.
  Rev. ed. of: Preaching and leading worship. c1984.
  Includes index.
  ISBN 978-0-664-23257-3 (alk. paper)
  1. Public worship. 2. Lord's Supper. 3. Baptism. 4. Preaching. I. Willimon, William H. Preaching and leading worship. II. Title.
  BV15.W535 2008
  264—dc22

                                                                        2007041695

*To those who preach and lead worship
in the churches of North Alabama*

Contents

Introduction

Pastor, preacher, administrator, teacher, counselor, interpreter, organizer—we clergy now wear so many hats, fill so many roles. No wonder we are often victims of vocational confusion, becoming sidetracked in our direction and allowing the nonessentials to elbow out the essentials in our parish work.

While we do not deny the importance of all the things we pastors do, there is one role we must do well or we are in big trouble. If our time and talent are not heavily invested in the tasks of preaching and worship leadership, our congregations are correct in assuming that we have lost the central focus of our ministry.

I say this for practical and theological reasons. Practically, preaching and worship leadership must be the center of a pastor's attention because the laity expect it. Every survey of lay expectations for clergy, particularly in Protestant churches, puts preaching at the top of the list. Studies of church growth confirm that churches do not grow without vibrant Sunday morning worship.

In Sunday preaching and worship, a pastor is present with the people of his or her congregation in a more intentional, explicit, and sustained manner than is possible in any other pastoral activity. Here is where the vast majority of our people will primarily know us as faithful, caring, competent pastors. Thus, any pastor who gives insufficient time and attention to his or her preaching and worship is simply not using time well, nor is he or she ministering to the needs of the laity.

Preaching and worship leadership are also central concerns for theological reasons. The Reformed tradition defines the church as the setting where "the Word is rightly preached and the sacraments are duly administered." The church is formed and reformed by these acts of faith. In the Roman Catholic tradition, Sunday worship is said to be "the summit toward which the activity of the Church is directed; at the same time it is the fountain from which all her power flows" (Constitution on the Sacred Liturgy, No. 10).

Here is the church in its most basic form as well as a pastor engaged in the most basic of pastoral tasks. This handbook is a practical guide to enable you to be an effective preacher and liturgist. Too much is at stake in the life of the church for us pastors to be anything less than competent, committed, and well-informed "servants of Christ and stewards of the mysteries of God" (1 Cor. 4:1).

1

Sunday Morning

Evaluating and Planning the Service

A flag, a handshake, a kiss. These are some of the daily rituals that encompass our lives. Ritual—patterned, predictable, purposeful behavior—makes life coherent, manageable, and meaningful.

Rituals enable us to encounter and to survive potentially threatening aspects of life—death, sex, birth, God. Sometimes people say, "We are too ritualistic in our church," as if ritual were an optional experience for Christians. But all human groups, particularly human groups that dare to approach the most mysterious parts of existence, live by ritual.

As a pastor, you know that our worship rituals are ambiguous phenomena. Our rites help us to encounter the holy. Sometimes they protect us from the holy! For instance, Christians celebrate the Lord's Supper—a ritual meal. What does this act mean? Paul says the Lord's Supper is *koinōnia*, Communion (1 Cor. 10:16–17). In this meal we commune with Christ and with one another. But our rituals for the Lord's Supper often conflict with *koinōnia*. Sitting in separate rows of pews, eating bits of bread, drinking from individual glasses— this is the rite of community?

So the question for the church is not whether we should worship through ritual, but *Will our rituals enable the church to do what it needs to do when it gathers to worship?* Time and again in our history, we have seen that rituals can be functional or dysfunctional. Our rites can edify us or enslave us. The way to reform bad rites is not simply to sweep them away, but rather to modify and replace them with more faithful liturgical expressions. Pastors are invariably reformers of worship, not because we believe in change for the sake of change, but because we know that these patterned stories, commands, symbols, gestures, and signs are the very source of our life and the test of our identity as Christians. These rites form or malform the church, so we should be attentive to what we are saying about the faith by what we do when we worship.

GUIDELINES FOR INNOVATION

The power of ritual is in its predictability and sameness. Ritual keeps calling and re-calling us to be attentive to what is important. Rituals must not be thoughtlessly tampered with, except for the best of reasons.

1. *Do not change a congregation's accustomed worship pattern until you have some clear understanding of the function of the accustomed patterns and unless you feel that the change is essential to preserving the vitality and fidelity of the congregation as people of God.* A good rule of thumb: make no major liturgical changes until you have served the congregation for at least a year.

2. *Never make liturgical changes solely at the pastor's discretion.* Include the laity in evaluating present practices, diagnosing problems, proposing the changes to be made, and evaluating whether the change should be a permanent part of your church's worship. Do your best to understand what the people get out of the present practice. Ask questions like, "You have been ushering here for many years. Tell me what your role is on Sunday morning."

3. *Be honest with yourself.* Ask yourself: Why do I want this change? Is it for purely personal matters of my own taste and liturgical preferences, or would this change truly benefit the corporate worship of this congregation? Everybody loses when liturgical innovation becomes a power struggle between the pastor and the people. As C. S. Lewis once said, "The charge is 'feed my sheep,' not 'run experiments on my rats.'"

4. *Use every means to explain the proposed change to the people.* Notes in the bulletin, a "rehearsal" before the service to help people feel more comfortable with the change, study groups in church school classes and other gatherings, even sermons can be ways to assure people that this change was proposed after much thought and for worthwhile reasons.

5. *Welcome comments on the changes.* Tell the congregation that you want to allow a reasonable period of time before a verdict is reached on whether or not the change should become a permanent part of the worship. The first few times we do something new in worship we usually don't like it simply because it is different and therefore uncomfortable.

6. *Introduce some innovation at a "special" service at a time other than Sunday morning.* For instance, a proposed change in the way your congregation celebrates Holy Communion might be received better at a Christmas Eve Communion service or on Maundy Thursday when people might expect and welcome something a bit different. If the change is well received, it may be introduced on a Sunday morning.

7. *Utilize the new worship resources of your own denomination in reforming your congregation's worship.* In most of our churches, there is little need for the pastor or Worship Committee to concoct special services individually. Few of us have the necessary verbal skills or historical and theological background required. Besides, your congregation has a right to expect that its worship will conform, at least in a general way, to the resources and expectations of your particular denominational heritage and expression of faith.

8. Finally, if your proposed liturgical changes are steadfastly resisted—even after your best attempts to involve the laity in

the planning, execution, and evaluation of those changes, even after your most skillful efforts to teach about those changes— *be willing to consider trying something else or backing off.* We only cling to and fight for those rituals that are important to us and functional for us. Sometimes misguided liturgical innovators have taken the worship away from the congregation, making the service over into their own clerical image of what ought to be, removing the liturgy from the forms and experiences of the congregation. This is a tragedy and the opposite of goals for innovation in the first place.

Now let us get down to specifics as we look at Sunday morning worship and the ways it can be improved.

In the past decade I have visited scores of Christian churches and conducted workshops and seminars for hundreds of pastors throughout the United States, Canada, and Australia. While many differences divide and distinguish the worship patterns of one church from those of another, there are a number of common weaknesses in our inherited worship patterns. These weaknesses are most common in Protestant churches (Roman Catholic parishes may have other problems). The needs may also differ from one socioeconomic situation to another because our worship is an intensely personal expression of who we are. Nevertheless, some generalizations can be made.

COMMON WEAKNESSES IN WORSHIP
AND HOW TO CORRECT THEM

1. *Lack of Focus and Coherence in the Acts of Worship.* The service moves in a dozen different directions at once. A hymn on the work of the Holy Spirit follows Scripture concerning the need for deeper dedication. The sermon calls for action. The anthem after the sermon speaks of Jesus as the one who soothes our worried souls. Careful planning is needed to correct this confusion. Two resources can help give direction to the service.

Many denominations now adhere to the time-honored practice of using *The Revised Common Lectionary* to determine which Scripture shall be read on Sunday. A lectionary is a table of selected Scripture lessons for each Sunday of the year. The ecumenical lectionary is on a three-year cycle of lessons that give an Old Testament, Epistle, and Gospel lesson for each Sunday, plus a psalm. The lections relate, at least in a general way, to the liturgical season of the year. In Advent, for instance, such themes as repentance, prophecy, and expectancy dominate the lessons. The lessons are usually selected on the basis of the Gospel lesson, though not always.

By using the lectionary as the starting point for your planning of the service, music, prayers, responses, sermon, and visuals can be coordinated with a general theme for the day.

Before the beginning of each liturgical season, I list the prescribed lessons for each Sunday in the pages of a notebook; then I read over the lessons in an attempt to discern a general theme that is suggested by one of the lessons. I jot this theme down on the page for that Sunday. This practice enables me to collect liturgical materials, ideas for a sermon, and hymns with this theme in mind.

The *church year*, a round of liturgical seasons, is another resource for planning. Many of our services not only lack coherence and direction but are also too much alike in emotional tone and in theological substance. The pastor rehashes the same pet themes, Sunday after Sunday, preaching from the same limited range of Scripture, singing the same tried-and-true hymns to the point of boredom. Our spiritual lives have variety—peaks and valleys, times of unrestrained joy and times of somber introspection. Corporate worship ought to reflect some of this variety and richness. If every Sunday is a day for giddy-headed joy or else for doleful lamentation, we are not forming our worship with the complexity of the content of the Bible itself. The church year, with its round of seasons on themes based on the life of Christ, preserves us from this boredom and sameness.

Without the aid of the church year, our Sundays could lose their focus on Christ and become a programmatic year in which the worship of God degenerates into a mere pep rally for the latest denominational cause or an expression of the pastor's personal whims. The church year includes the full sweep of Christ's life and teaching. As the colors change with each season (Advent, purple or blue; Christmas, white; Epiphany, green; Lent, purple; Easter, white; Pentecost, red), so also each season changes our focus, our perspective on the gospel. The gospel is a multifaceted jewel. The church year enables us to experience all sides of this jewel in their brilliance.

Advent anticipates the coming and coming again of Christ. During the four Sundays before Christmas, we prepare ourselves for the mystery of God coming to reign among us.

Christmas is the joyous festival of Christ's incarnation, extending to Epiphany (January 6).

Epiphany celebrates the revelation of Christ as the Savior of the world, even as he was revealed to the visiting Magi of old. During Epiphany, the mission and outreach of the church are emphasized.

Lent is the forty-day period beginning on Ash Wednesday and continuing until Easter. Lent is a time of self-examination, self-discipline, and focus on the realities of human sin that made the cross inevitable as God's loving response to our sin.

Holy Week begins with Palm Sunday, the day of Jesus' triumphal entry into Jerusalem. On Maundy Thursday we remember the night he gathered with his disciples to observe the Last Supper. Good Friday is the somber day of commemoration of the crucifixion.

Easter joy contrasts with the previous days of Lent. Easter is the fifty-day season of joyful celebration of Christ's resurrection and reflection upon its meaning for us today.

Pentecost begins a season that some churches call "Ordinary Time." After the day when the church was born by an outpouring of the Holy Spirit at Pentecost, there begins a long, orderly reflection upon the various themes of Christian belief.

Among the different denominations, there has always been variation in which days of the church year are celebrated in particular ways. But in your congregation, the church year and the lectionary can be wonderful resources for planning a service in which all the various acts and media of worship are coordinated to give focus and direction to the service.

The lectionary also enables a pastor to give the lessons to musicians so that they too can plan in advance in accordance with the themes of the day. Most volunteer choirs must begin rehearsing for their choral music many weeks before they sing it in the service. It is embarrassing that many choir directors know what their choirs will be singing two months ahead while their pastor doesn't know what he or she will be preaching next Sunday!

It is wise for a pastor to meet with the music leaders and plan services a few months in advance. If the worship leaders see liturgical planning as a team effort, the service will automatically be more unified. In the last chapter of this book we discuss how a worship planning and evaluation committee might function in a parish.

2. *Inadequate Treatment of Scripture.* A few years ago we did a survey in my denomination and found that, in the majority of United Methodist churches, only one Scripture lesson was read each Sunday. Seventy-five percent of the time that lesson would be from one of the four Gospels. Yet we, like most Protestants, think of ourselves as a church that keeps the Bible central. We must expose God's people to a wider array of Scripture on Sunday mornings.

Once again, the three-year ecumenical lectionaries can be helpful here. While the lectionary is an excellent resource for biblical preaching, the main purpose of the lectionary is to facilitate the orderly reading of Scripture. We believe that the Bible contains God's Word—whether the Bible is preached from on Sunday morning or not.

Many of us must admit that we have used a limited canon on Sunday morning—mostly our favorite texts, which we use as a springboard for a sermon. Three lessons read from the lectionary every Sunday will give the people a new confrontation with the Word. When we read more Scripture, we may have to take more care in the way we read the Scripture so that the people can appreciate its full significance. The use of trained, talented lay readers of Scripture is one way to make sure that the reading of Scripture is exposure to the true and lively Word.

One by-product of the new lectionaries is an increasing number of Christian educational materials and devotional resources that are keyed to a lectionary, which provides a linking of family devotional time or church school study sessions with Sunday worship. Check your denominational resources for the availability of such materials.

By the way, in the order of worship, the Scripture should immediately precede the sermon. When the Scripture is read early in the service, perhaps twenty minutes before the sermon, there is no apparent relationship between the read word and the preached word. When linked closely, the preaching and reading of the Bible are seen as reciprocal activities that nourish the church.

3. *Inadequate Opportunities for Congregational Participation and Response.* Many of the Sunday orders of worship feel like performances with the pastor speaking, the pastor praying, the pastor reading, and the choir singing, with little opportunity for the congregation to do anything but sit and listen.

The gospel message entails response to the Word, embodiment, incarnation. The gospel movement is incomplete without a response, a clear yes, in word and deed. When the Sunday service is simply a time to sit quietly, hear some good music and a good sermon, sing a hymn, and then go home to eat dinner, no wonder many of our people get confused into thinking that Christ only wants passive admirers rather than active followers.

What is true for the pastor is also true for the choir. Throughout the history of Christian worship, there has been a recurring tendency of choirs to take the music away from the congregation. The most appropriate function of the choir is to aid the congregation's music rather than perform for the congregation, to help make the *congregation* the choir. Many new anthems have the choir sing the more difficult parts and then have the congregation join in on the easier parts. Choirs can also help teach the congregation new hymns.

Laypersons can share in the leadership of the service—by reading Scripture, making announcements, leading prayers, and receiving the offering. Some acts such as preaching or blessing are appropriately reserved for the pastor, not necessarily because the pastor is any more adept at doing these things than the rest of us but because, when the pastor does these things, he or she does them as the representative, the official, of the whole church.

More acts of worship need to be placed after the sermon as our response to the reading and preaching of the Word. In past times, many congregations came to think of acts of worship like the pastoral prayer, the offering, the creed, and the anthem as mere preliminaries. And why not? We put all these acts early in the service, as little warm-up exercises to get us ready for the main event of the sermon. But what if we reclaimed these acts as *response* to the Word rather than preparation for the Word?

4. Insufficient Attention to the Acts of Gathering for Worship. If the people in the congregation have not seen each other during the past week, if there are things we need to do and say in order to assemble and focus ourselves in order to worship, these should be done in a time of gathering before the service begins.

If announcements are to be made, they should be made at this time, not in the middle of the service. You need not be embarrassed about beginning with announcements. This listing of the weekly activities and opportunities for service helps to underscore the need for the time of worship to be a time of motivation and renewal.

If new or unaccustomed acts of worship will be done during the service, the gathering would be a good time for an informal rehearsal. It is never appropriate to surprise a congregation with a totally unfamiliar hymn tucked within the service. We all desperately need to increase our repertoire of familiar hymns. Musicians in the congregation could help the rest of us learn the hymn during a time of rehearsal. Here the pastor could share some of the meaning of the hymn and the rationale for asking the congregation to learn this new music.

The gathering is also the best time to greet visitors. When

guests come to your home, you don't wait until thirty minutes after they have entered before you welcome and introduce them. The creation of a friendly, warm congregational setting where everyone knows what is happening and everyone feels welcome is an essential prerequisite for meaningful worship.

5. *Architectural Setting Not Always Conducive to the Type of Worship Climate We Wish to Create.* Many of us are burdened by this problem on Sunday morning, which is not a part of the order of worship but which may have a powerful effect. Take a moment and look at your worship space as if you were a newcomer. What does the architectural setting say to you? Does it speak of drabness, clutter, confusion of focus, neglect? Does your eye move naturally to a point of attention? Do worshipers and leaders have room to move about? Where is the focus for baptism or the Lord's Supper?

The architectural setting exercises a powerful though subtle influence upon us. Much of our worship does not work, not because we have planned or executed the service poorly but because the building works against our liturgical goals. We try to create a warm, hospitable atmosphere for our meeting, but the cold, dark, formalized building with heavy, forbidding furniture and row upon row of bolted-down pews works against us and shouts down any other point we are trying to make in our liturgy. Perhaps the clutter from the praise band makes it appear that we are unconcerned about the visual appearance of the worship space.

You may have inherited a building which makes a theological statement that was adequate for the past but which no longer suits contemporary visions of faithfulness. The use of an older building can be one of the most trying liturgical challenges a pastor faces. Creativity is required. An architectural consultant or designer could be helpful. The pastor and worship committee should look critically at their building and note what the design keeps them from doing on Sunday morning. Then the consultant could make suggestions for modifications.

While the alteration of a beloved old building can be a traumatic experience for a congregation, it may be essential if the congregation is to embody new liturgical expressions sufficiently. Sometimes all that is required is the removal of some superfluous fixtures and furniture, or the introduction of new lighting techniques or color.

Generally speaking, the architectural space for contemporary worship should be light, open, uncluttered, adaptable, inviting, and warm, and it should provide for the audibility and visibility of worship leaders.

6. *Exclusion of Children.* In many mainline Protestant denominations, children have recently become a "problem" in our worship. As worship became more didactic—more verbally oriented and less action oriented—as music became more difficult to sing, and as the congregation became more passive, congregations complained that their children did not get anything out of Sunday worship. Of course, many of these worship patterns also excluded some adults who found it difficult to concentrate through a thirty-minute sermon, to sing the more sophisticated hymns, and to worship in a service that had become dull and formalized. Children are incapable of thinking in abstract concepts until late adolescence, so they were left out of the sermon—and so were many adults.

Some churches tried to solve the problem of children in worship by concocting "children's sermons," "children's church," and other devices to interest the children. I feel that most of these efforts are misguided. Many so-called children's sermons are neither sermons nor are they for children. They are usually petty, unscriptural, moralistic object lessons that children find difficult to follow because they cannot make the connection between the object and the lesson. The children's sermon is often for the parents—the preacher telling the children what Mommy and Daddy believe the children ought to hear. Younger children cannot understand the moralisms put forth in the children's sermon, and older children refuse to come forward for the children's sermon because they feel that they are being put on display and made to look foolish—which they often are. By having a children's sermon the church says, in effect, "Children, you are incapable of worshiping with the church. The service is incomprehensible or irrelevant to you."

Children at any age *can* worship. They may not worship in the same way or at the same cognitive level as adults, but they still worship. Fortunately, being a Christian is not entirely a cognitive matter. It is also a matter of affections, symbol, story, and mystery. Most of us became Christian not by thinking about the faith and making rational decisions about Christ, but rather by simply watching our elders and then growing into faith in a natural way, the way we inherited most of our important values. How odd that we should attempt to reach children through the sermon when we know that other acts of worship—music, sacraments, actions—would be more appropriate for their stage of development.

Many of our worship practices (our abstract sermons, long prayers, and passive worship) need to be changed in order to accommodate the needs of children—and adults. Pastors who are told by their congregations, "We get more out of your children's sermon than from your regular sermon," ought to take the hint. This statement says more about the incomprehensibility of their sermons than about the value of children's sermons.

Very young children may be kept in the church nursery, but as soon as possible the church needs to let parents and children know that they belong in our Sunday worship. Parents may need to develop skills in keeping children occupied or diverted during the parts of the service when children may get restless. One church provides activity boxes for preschool children. A child upon entering the sanctuary can select an activity—a coloring book, a Bible story book, a doll—to play with. The item is returned at the end of the service. Some churches hand out children's leaflets, available from a number of church supply houses, that provide stories and activities keyed to the Scripture lessons for that Sunday.

Jesus gave little children a key place in his kingdom. We must work to restore children to a key place in our worship.

7. *Poor Formation and Leadership of Public Prayer.* Chapter 3 is devoted to the renewal of public prayer. When our prayers in

church are full of clichés and hackneyed, vague phrases, what are we teaching the people about prayer? For many, Sunday worship is seen as a time to listen to the preacher deliver the sermon. But what if we began to conceive of our worship as an occasion for prayer, a time to lift our souls in one heart and voice to God? Sunday would be seen in the way that the church primarily saw its worship for most of the centuries—as a time for the people to listen and speak to God rather than a time for the people to listen to the preacher.

8. *Many Free-Church Protestants Are Guilty of a Woeful Neglect of Baptism and the Lord's Supper.* How can we call our worship biblically based when we haphazardly and halfheartedly celebrate the Lord's Supper only a few times during the year and when we rush through baptism as an unimportant intrusion into our worship? We go into more detail concerning the renewal of the sacraments and ordinances in chapter 4.

Children learn by doing and seeing. So do adults. Perhaps Jesus knew this. He didn't just preach the gospel, he enacted the gospel around the table of friends. Jesus invited sinners not just to feel something in their hearts, but to join in the banquet, to follow him actively. As John Calvin says, God remembers that we are creatures, and so the Creator loves us in ways we can understand—in bread and wine and water. These actions of faith are too deep for words, as are most important experiences of life.

Christian worship is faith in action, belief performed and embodied in word and in deed.

2

The Service

Effective Liturgical Leadership

Many of our common weaknesses in Sunday morning worship have their root in an inadequate pattern or order of worship. In this chapter we discuss a suggested pattern for Sunday worship as well as some of the essentials of good liturgical leadership.

A PATTERN FOR SUNDAY WORSHIP

An ecumenical consensus is emerging that a full service of Word *and* Table is the normal Sunday morning activity for Christians. The majority of the world's Christians celebrate and always have celebrated this full service. The Reformers, particularly Luther, Calvin, and Wesley, intended their followers to celebrate the Lord's Supper every Sunday. A strange irony of liturgical history is that the reform movement, which set out to restore the Eucharist to the laity, was to result, in spite of the Reformers' intentions, in nearly removing the Lord's Supper from the laity altogether. The emergent church is recovering the joy of sacramental worship for a new generation.

Our problem as free-church Protestants is that we have

attempted to make the service of the Word bear the total burden of the congregation's judgment, grace, healing, nourishment, response, and edification. Although the sermon is a key
worship activity (and I talk about improving our preaching in
chapters 5, 6, and 7), we pastors are cheating our people when
we do not move from the Word to the Table. Congregational
response is a major problem for those of us who do not use the
full Word and Table pattern, because congregational movement to the Lord's Table is *the* primary, biblical, historical
response to the read, prayed, and preached Word.

While an individual congregation could give much variety
to the content of each act, a basic pattern that honors the people's need for ritual and predictability in worship should be followed. The content of the pattern may vary in accordance with
the variations within the church year, the Scripture for the day,
or congregational concerns.

For instance, the basic pattern opens with the *gathering of
the church*. But there are as many different ways to gather as
there are congregations. One Sunday the congregation might
gather with a choral call to worship. Another Sunday the gathering might be a time for everyone to shake hands.

Here is a recommended pattern:

A BASIC PATTERN OF WORSHIP

THE SERVICE OF THE WORD

Gathering of the Church

The people of God come together. Announcements, greet-
ings, music, song, opening prayer, and processions are
included here.

Proclamation and Praise

The Scriptures are read to the people. Preaching follows,
along with anthems, songs, hymns, and other acts of worship that proclaim God's Word and praise God's name.

Responses and Offerings

Having heard the Word, the people respond through acts of commitment such as prayers, gifts, and service for the world and to one another.

THE SERVICE OF THE TABLE

Taking of the Bread and the Cup

On those Sundays when the Lord's Supper is celebrated (and we hope they will be more frequent) we now move to the Table. Having heard and responded to the Word, we enact the Word according to our Lord's command. As Jesus took the bread and the cup, so do we.

The Great Thanksgiving

As Jesus gave thanks over the bread and the cup, so do we in this historic prayer, which lifts up the full sweep of salvation history culminating in the ritual of the upper room and in the other meals of Jesus' ministry.

Breaking the Bread

As Jesus broke the bread, so do we in this vivid act.

Giving the Bread and the Cup

As Jesus gave the bread and the cup to his disciples in this act of love, so we share the bread and the cup with one another. This dynamic of giving and receiving is a sign of the Christian life and of what God has done for us in Jesus Christ. Then we scatter into the world, nourished and blessed.

Compare this pattern with the one currently in use in your congregation and the ones that your denomination recommends. By following this pattern, or something close to it, we enable our people to experience the fullness of biblical worship.

On Sundays when we do not celebrate the service of the Table (and, realistically, I expect that will be the majority of Sundays in many of our Protestant churches for some time to come), the service simply ends after the various responses (a creed, the offering, an anthem, the pastoral prayer, and the final hymn) are made. In this pattern we fulfill the ancient word: "And they devoted themselves to the apostles' teaching and fellowship, to the breaking of bread and the prayers" (Acts 2:42).

THE GRACIOUS HOST

In the Word and Table pattern the leader of worship might think of himself or herself as host at a meal. The gracious host makes people feel comfortable, welcomed, prepared for. The good host knows that in order for people to feel comfortable they need someone in charge, someone to give them the direction they need in order to participate fully. Many services of worship are ruined by a leader who mumbles through the service, remains hidden behind the furniture, chatters too much, gives little or no direction to the congregation, or stumbles through the service in a manner that makes everyone uncomfortable.

The pastor sets the tone for the liturgical assembly. If a pastor approaches the Sunday service in a halfhearted way, halfhearted worship is the result. Enthusiasm (literally, filled with the divine Spirit) is contagious—so are nervousness, boredom, and fatigue.

Effective liturgical leadership is partly a matter of using our God-given gifts and natural abilities—physical appearance, voice, intelligence. But effective liturgical leadership is also a matter (perhaps more than we would like to admit) of the intentional, lifelong development of leadership skills.

1. *Preparation.* Good worship is premeditated. *Long-term preparation* involves a clear understanding of what we want to happen in our worship, and a basic knowledge of the theology behind our prayer, praise, preaching, and the Sacraments. It also involves getting to know the congregation.

Your presence in congregational crises, issues, and achievements provides the basic material for congregational prayer and praise. The planning and execution of a good worship experience on Sunday morning is not simply a matter of moving through a certain liturgical order. It is also a matter of seeing that the activities are appropriate for this people at this time and place in order to be fully open to the leading of the Holy Spirit.

Immediate preparation involves immersion in the spirit of the liturgical season, in the lessons for that season, and in the contemporary concerns of the church. During the season of Lent our worship should have a tone recognizably different from what it will have during Easter. Our restrained, subdued manner during Lenten services will contrast with the joy and exuberance of our leadership style at Easter.

Spend time immediately before the service focusing on the service. Look over the order of worship, reflect on the prayers and the Scripture lessons, and think about the sermon. Picture the individuals who will be gathering for this service. What needs will they bring to this gathering? What would you like to happen today? Liturgical preparation is a form of prayer.

Be sure to have all the materials ready for when you need them during the service. Mark the prayers and hymns you will be using in your hymnal or worshipbook. Many times our nervousness and awkwardness are related to our knowledge that we are not adequately prepared for this service.

Whenever you are going to do something unusual, practice is necessary. A visit to the choir during their rehearsal is a good way to cue in a few people in the congregation about a change in the service. This action also helps the choir to see themselves as fellow leaders in the service.

2. *Style. Remember that worship leadership is a visual as well as an auditory experience for the congregation.* The major weakness of most Protestant worship leaders whom I have observed is their failure to be sensitive to the body language they are sending to the congregation. What is your physical appearance? Are your vestments in good order? Does your posture

speak of your enthusiasm or of your fatigue? All pastors need a full-length mirror so they can check themselves before entering the worship area.

The most effective liturgical leadership is by sight rather than by sound. A good leader doesn't need to chatter throughout the service, telling people every move to make. Gestures are much more appropriate. Liturgical direction should be given with confident, flowing gestures. You should be visible to the entire congregation at all times. It is disconcerting for the congregation to view a jack-in-the-box as the leader pops in and out of the woodwork or from behind some oversized piece of furniture. People are dependent upon you for direction. For instance, during an anthem your full attention should be on the choir. (It is not a time to get your notes together or to tie your shoe.) Your attention helps the wandering eyes of the congregation to focus appropriately on the action of the moment. If your choir is visible to the congregation, choir members also need reminding that they are not to talk, move about, or search for music while other liturgical action is taking place. The choir's focus helps the congregation to move as one and to see that each act of worship is important.

Your eyes are the principal means of exercising liturgical leadership. When someone else is leading the congregation, your eyes should be on that person. When you are leading, your eyes should attempt to touch as many individuals as possible. When you hand someone a piece of bread in the Communion, your eyes should focus on that person alone in a way that is immediate and intimate.

Keep custody of your tongue. Most of us need to give less verbal direction in our leadership and more visual direction. Our liturgies are too wordy already. Sometimes in our nervousness we get into a bad habit of chattering, covering all acts with a profusion of words: "Now let's all open our hymnals and turn with me to that great and familiar hymn of Charles Wesley, 'Love divine, all loves excelling, Joy of heaven, to earth come down.' Let us stand as we sing."

People need space in the service, space to be quiet, space to think, space to feel, space to be left alone with God—without the preacher's constant barrage of verbiage. This custody of the tongue, like many other aspects of our leadership, requires conscious self-discipline for most of us.

While Sunday worship is generally not the best time for long periods of silent meditation and introspection—Sunday is a corporate, communal celebration, a time to get together rather than a time to be alone—short periods of silence can be helpful times of focus and worship as well as a way to underscore our acts of speech and music. Moments of silence are not intermissions. The presider can encourage an appreciation of these periods of silence by allowing enough time for them to become real. At first the congregation may feel a bit awkward—they have been so accustomed to wordy, hectic worship patterns—but your posture and attitude during the silence help them use silence to better advantage. Appropriate times for silence: immediately before a prayer of intercession, as a time of centering thoughts before a time of communication; after the Scripture is read, as a time of personal reflection; any other time when quiet will underscore the function of the liturgy at that moment.

Now let's take it from the top and identify specific leadership attitudes and skills that are required to lead a congregation through this suggested pattern for Sunday worship.

PRESIDING IN THE PATTERN

1. *Gathering of the Church.* The tone for the service is set here. Prepare people for any unusual aspects of the service. Greet visitors without embarrassing them. Keep your announcements and rehearsal *short.*

2. *Proclamation and Praise.* Choir leaders should direct the choir as unobtrusively as possible.

When the Scriptures are read, open the Bible and turn to the lessons. A substantial, finely bound Bible should be used—no paperbacks or paraphrased versions, please—a good, formal contemporary translation is best. There is no need to announce chapter and verse of a reading, particularly if that information is printed in the worship bulletin. "The Epistle is from the First Letter to the Corinthians" is sufficient. However, sometimes a *few* sentences of introduction to the text may be given, such as: "Paul is writing these words to a bitterly divided church. In chiding them for their divisions, Paul says. . . ." No one should read Scripture in public who has not practiced reading the passage aloud, in front of a mirror, and who cannot be heard by everyone. A moment of silence may be observed immediately after the Scripture is read.

We discuss sermon preparation and delivery in subsequent chapters.

3. *Responses and Offerings.* If a creed is used as a response, it should be led in a strong, affirmative manner. Observe a moment of silence before the prayer so that the people have time to get themselves in a suitable frame of mind. If the Peace (a gesture of embrace before the offering) is to be exchanged, the presider sets the example by greeting the other ministers or a few members of the congregation in a firm, warm embrace. If the minister communicates naturalness in this greeting, the people will respond in kind. Don't allow the Peace to drag. You are responsible for sensing when an act of worship has ended and the group needs to move on.

The offering is announced by the presider in full view of the people, by saying something like: "Let us offer ourselves and our gifts to God." Ushers should be trained to move efficiently but not impersonally or hurriedly in collecting the gifts. Then the offering is brought forward, perhaps with some appropriately joyous music, such as a doxology, and placed upon the altar. It is symbolically absurd either to pray *before* the offering is received or to neglect to place the offering on the table once it is collected. The offering, a fitting act of response after the proclamation, is an important sign that the people should not miss.

4. *The Taking, Thanking, Breaking, and Giving at the Lord's Table.* Much needs to be said about the pastor's leadership at

the Table, but we reserve comment on the special skills required for this part of the service until chapter 4.

The service ends (whether we move to the Table or simply end with other responses after the sermon) with the blessing or benediction. In this final act of worship, the pastor blesses the people before they scatter. The blessing is not a prayer; it is a farewell word from the pastor to the congregation in God's name. Therefore it should be done audibly in front of the congregation, with arms outstretched as if to embrace the congregation, or with hands raised over the people. After the people are blessed, it is appropriate for them to respond with a spoken or sung amen. Then the pastor may move to the door to bid farewell to worshipers as they leave.

CEREMONIAL ACTS

Because actions speak louder than words, we must be sensitive to our ceremonial acts, as sensitive as we are to the words we use in prayer or praise. Here are a few guidelines:

1. *Our actions should highlight the important aspects of our worship.* We light the candles as a sign that worship is beginning. We put the offering plates upon the altar as a sign of our self-giving to the God who has given so selflessly to all. We handle the Bible with care and ceremony before we read it to emphasize that this book is the source of our common life.

2. *Our actions should relate to the size of the building.* The bigger the worship space, the more articulate and definite should be the physical gestures used.

3. *Our actions should relate to the style of the worship space.* Some buildings are formal and dignified; casual, folksy leadership styles don't work there. Other buildings are open, modern, and warm. Some worship styles violate the integrity of the context. Nothing is worse than a worship leader whose style seems to turn some beautiful old Gothic cathedral into a little rural church or, on the other hand, to turn a familial, warm rural church into some formal, aloof downtown cathedral.

4. Likewise, *the size of the congregation makes a difference in how we lead them.* We don't need to speak to the balcony in a church where only fifty people are present—all downstairs. We need not ask for personal, spoken prayer requests in a church where four hundred people are gathered.

5. *The nature of the congregation also influences how we lead them.* Who are these people? What do they regard as irreverent? What is their median age, educational level, and past liturgical experience?

6. *The relative importance of the day makes a difference in our leadership style.* If we do everything in a big way every Sunday, how do we celebrate truly special days? The church formerly did not sing alleluias during Lent nor did it allow kneeling during Easter. Processionals with the clergy and choir might be reserved for particularly festive Sundays.

7. Finally, *our own personalities affect how we lead.* Ask yourself, Can I do this with ease, conviction, and unself-consciously? Don't baptize a baby until you have learned to hold a baby in a gracious manner. Don't call the children to the front for a children's sermon if you are basically uncomfortable with young children. Some gestures can be learned; others violate our limitations and abilities.

VESTMENTS

Some clergy today dress casually in order to lead worship. They believe it is important to set a casual tone in their contemporary congregations. Their casual dress is not a statement about the unimportance of clergy dress, but its importance.

Christian clergy have traditionally worn vestments as a way of distinguishing who is leading the liturgy. Vestments help to accentuate that the clergy functions here not as an individual person, but as the representative of the whole group. The particular vestment worn depends on your denominational tradition as well as the style and tradition of your congregation. Protestant ministers have traditionally worn either a black academic gown or a white surplice over a black cassock. The alb, a full-length white vestment girded at the waist with a ropelike belt called a cincture, has become very popular. Traditionally, the alb was simply a basic garment of the Roman people. Later it became associated with the celebration of the service of Holy Communion. Many clergy have adopted the alb because it gives a brighter, lighter effect than the somber black robe and because it fits somewhat more snugly to the body rather than simply enveloping the body. This observation reminds us that vestments are primarily a visual, emotional matter. Therefore, selection of vestments will be as much a matter of taste and visual effect as a matter of church tradition.

Ordained ministers may wear a stole over the alb or surplice. This long narrow piece of cloth was originally a sort of necktie or symbol of rank in Roman society. The stole is generally keyed to the liturgical color of the season, though, once again, color is primarily an emotional matter rather than a rational one. Does it make sense to wear purple during Lent as a sign of penitence? Do people still think of penitence when they see purple? Traditionally, there was much variation and local adaptation took place within the liturgical color scheme—and it may do so today.

If there are other vested clergy during a service, the presiding minister may be distinguished by wearing a chasuble (a loose-fitting, poncholike garment) at the Eucharist, or a cope over the alb or surplice on occasions when the Eucharist is not celebrated.

In the past, a great deal of allegorical symbolism was attached to various vestments. Most of the vestments began as parts of the standard formal dress of the day and were retained in later years as special dress for clergy. Today in the Protestant Church, vestments are worn not because of some theological meaning behind each piece of clothing but because they add beauty and dignity to the worship service. Traditional vestments provide a visible sign of continuity with the church of ages past. They remind the congregation that they are participating in something older than the contemporary congregation. They are also a sign of the church's catholicity, its participation in the universal church of Christ.

SHARING LEADERSHIP WITH THE LAITY

Laypeople should be actively recruited for leadership in the Sunday service. Their participation reinforces the belief in the priesthood of believers and becomes a sign of what the laity do throughout the week: assist the pastor in caring for the congregation so that the congregation can fulfill its ministry in the world.

But laypeople must be trained for their leadership. Sunday worship is too important for anyone to spoil it for the rest because that person is improperly equipped for the role we ask him or her to perform. Generally speaking, the guidelines we have given for pastors as worship leaders should apply to laity as well. Use these guidelines in training laypersons to be readers of Scripture, ushers, musicians, acolytes, crucifers, servers of Communion, sponsors in baptism, and participants in other leadership tasks that the pastor may share with the laity. No leadership task need be reserved exclusively for the ordained clergy except those tasks that an ordained minister needs to do as a representative sign of the whole church. Usually this means that the pastor should be the one to preach, offer prayers of intercession, pronounce forgiveness after a prayer of confession, pray the prayer of thanksgiving at the Lord's Supper, baptize, and bless at the end of the service.

3

Public Prayer

Speaking and Listening to God

Corporate worship is essentially an act of common prayer. As we noted earlier, many of us Protestants have conceived of worship as preaching and listening to preaching. While we in no way want to denigrate preaching, we want to see preaching as one act of worship within the context of many acts of dialogue between God and God's people in worship.

Many Christians today have forgotten how to pray. They say that God is absent from their lives, far away, silent. What they may be saying is that *they* have become absent from God, silent. They may not be hearing God because they have not disciplined themselves to listen. They may not be able to speak to God because they have not learned the necessary skills in communicating with the Creator.

One function of Sunday worship is to teach us all to pray, even as Jesus taught his disciples to pray. (Interestingly, prayer is the only thing the disciples asked Jesus to teach them.) Every Sunday the church says in effect: "Do you want to know how to speak to God? Then come join us in our efforts on Sunday morning. Before long, you will get the hang of it and will be able to speak to God yourself whenever you want to. Here, on

Sunday morning, we learn by doing. We experiment with and then internalize the patterns by which we speak and listen to the God who is also speaking and listening to us."

The primary function of worship is to glorify and to enjoy God. But while we are doing this, we are also being formed into a certain sort of people who think and behave in certain ways. We are learning through liturgy, growing in our faith—a gracious by-product of our worship of God. So pastors would do well to ask, "What are we teaching our people about prayer through our prayer on Sunday morning?"

Not long ago, one of my parishioners told me that he was being harassed at work by an unscrupulous supervisor. The supervisor wanted to see the man hounded out of his job, so he did everything possible to humiliate him and make his life miserable.

"I hate him. I am afraid that one day at work he will push me too far and I will pick up a wrench and bash his brains out," the parishioner told me.

We talked about his feelings toward the supervisor, and I suggested that he might pray each morning before going to work, asking God to help him endure this man's attacks.

"I never thought about prayer," he said.

"Oh, yes. Jesus urges us to bless our enemies and to pray for those who persecute us," I added.

"I never heard us pray for enemies on Sunday morning," he said.

It hit me. What had this man learned about prayer on Sunday morning? Had he learned that prayer was a spiritual resource, an integral part of everyday life, an essential aspect of our relationship to God? He had probably learned that prayer is irrelevant to the really pressing needs of life; prayer is nothing but vague, religious-sounding, hackneyed clichés. The Anglican *Book of Common Prayer* contains prayers for enemies, rain, national leaders, the birth of a 'child, peace, humility, and all the other nitty-gritty concerns of life. In so doing, it helps to make our prayer truly *common* prayer—a common part of the common life of the people of God. This is the goal for our prayer on Sunday morning. If a congregation's prayers are exclusively concerned with members of the congregation who are ill, that congregation needs a more biblical, more expansive practice of Christian prayer.

PRAYING IN PUBLIC

It is important to make a distinction between public and private prayer. Private prayer appears to be of growing interest among many of our people. The Christian social activist who could have said a decade ago, "My work is my prayer," has found that spiritual bankruptcy is the result of a failure to keep at prayer. Many people today are experimenting with various forms of private prayer in their individual prayer life, but private and public prayer are different. Jesus participated in the prayers of the synagogue, but he also had his lonely times apart. We find both modes of prayer in the Old and New Testaments and in the history of the liturgy. One is not superior to the other; in fact they are complementary ways of being in the presence of God.

What is public prayer? First, *public prayer is not private prayer said publicly.* For those of us in the so-called free churches (Baptist, Methodist, Presbyterian, Pentecostal, etc.) the confusion of these two modes of prayer has been harmful to public worship. Private prayer is a kind of no-holds-barred, divine-human encounter. It is important to engage in it often, to keep at it, and to express everything on one's mind. It is like a private, intimate conversation with a best friend. It doesn't matter what is said as long as it is the honest cry of the heart. Probably in private prayer there is a need to do less talking and more listening, but that is another matter! While certain methods of meditation and reflection can be helpful, there are few rules for private prayer except to be oneself and to have the courage to let God be God.

But public prayer is different. When a minister leads a prayer in the midst of corporate worship, that pastor must not offer his or her own prayer. Your job as the pastor is not to give the people your prayer but rather to lead them in their prayer. Your innermost longings, your personal doubts and prejudices may be interesting, but they are not interesting here. The only reason you are given the privilege (or the burden, depending on how you look at it) to be in front of the congregation at this moment is to lead the congregation in prayer. They want to pray, not to be dazzled by your ability to form beautiful phrases or to be embarrassed by your inability to speak clearly and meaningfully. Your personal concerns and innermost feelings have a place in your leadership of corporate prayer only as they are related to the corporate concerns of the congregation. Your function, in the leadership of prayer, is that of a conductor or coach rather than that of the lead actor or soloist.

The worship leader must lead without standing in the way of worship, without becoming a liturgical virtuoso, a prima donna of prayer to the point that the people cannot see God because they are too busy admiring you! Good public prayers do not call attention to themselves. They become vehicles for communication with God rather than performances for the crowd.

Not only does public prayer differ in character from private prayer, but there are also different types of public prayer. We Protestants have long debated the merits of "free" versus "liturgical" prayer or "extemporaneous" versus "written" prayer. Now, as with any act of worship, it is not a matter of "formal" versus "informal" prayer. There is really no such thing as an "informal" prayer. Whenever two or more people are gathered, they must use some agreed-upon form if they are to communicate. They use language, grammar, gestures, and other forms that give meaning to what they say and make what they say comprehensible to someone else.

If you ask me to stand up at a worship gathering and pray extemporaneously, I will be forced to use certain forms or my prayer will sound like gibberish to you. I will use the English language and, because I am a Christian, I will use special words, names, symbols, and standard endings and beginnings which are the form peculiar to this faith. So the real issue is not liturgical versus free prayer or formal versus informal prayer. The issue is whether or not our forms are functional or dysfunctional, whether they do an adequate job of communicating for the congregation.

Which form of prayer is more adequate for public prayer? Unfortunately, we often have taken sides on two extreme ends of the question. Those of us who are part of the Puritan tradition have upheld the value of free, spontaneous prayer "from the heart." But we should remember that the Puritans never committed themselves to one form of prayer. Though the more radical Puritans repudiated all preconceived prayers, and some even repudiated the use of the Lord's Prayer in worship, the Westminster Directory of 1644, the Puritan worship guide, provides for *both* written and free prayers. The free-church tradition advocates a positive rather than a negative freedom. We are free to make use of the rich heritage of the church's historical prayers and free to construct new prayers of our own. The historic Protestant position has been that there is value in both types of prayer in public worship.

What are the comparative strengths and weaknesses of liturgical and free prayer? First, *liturgical prayer* has the virtue of saving the congregation from the individual minister's moods and abilities. Corporate prayer is too important to be left exclusively to the whims and talents of one person, even if that person is professionally trained and ordained. Ordered, carefully worded, historic prayers give objectivity and stability to the service, catholicity, scriptural soundness, historical awareness, and continuity with the prayers of the church at all times and places.

The value of using prayers from a worshipbook, hymnal, or church bulletin is that the people can participate to the fullest extent. They are enabled to anticipate what is coming, follow the words for themselves, and return to the prayer later if they wish so that the "Amen" will be their true response. Printed prayers serve the same purpose as printed music in the hymnal: so that everyone can get into the act, so that all can be together.

There are defects in liturgical prayer. Does this type of prayer leave room for the promptings of the Holy Spirit? (Romans 8:26 says that the Spirit helps us to pray.) These general prayers are often just that—general. They lack particularity, contemporaneity, specificity. This form of prayer can indeed slip into cold, lifeless formalism.

As for *free prayer,* it provides for the intuitive, spontaneous, pastoral gathering of the prayers of the people, linking us to that free, charismatic, apostolic prayer of the early church. Free prayer enables speaking to be the particular speech of this particular congregation in this particular time and place. We thus move our prayer from the abstract to the concrete, from the general to the specific—a necessary movement in an incarnational faith that deals with concrete specifics.

But free prayer also has its defects. For one thing, so many of our public prayers are rarely free or extemporaneous. One of the biggest problems on Sunday morning is the long prayer or pastoral prayer. I have asked congregations, "If I were to give you pencil and paper, could you write out your pastor's prayer for next Sunday?" Most of them say they could. Many of our pastoral prayers are a maze of poorly thought-out, confusing clichés; hackneyed expressions; shallow constructions; and formalized, impersonal ramblings. The danger of the spontaneous prayer delivered by the pastor is that the congregation will be at the mercy of the minister's moods. There will be too much focus on the pastor's personal concerns and too little attention to the whole range of Christian concern. The prayer will not be corporate prayer but rather the pastor's idiosyncratic ramblings.

Much of what we call "pastoral prayer" has two problems: it is not pastoral, that is, it is not the prayer of someone who knows and speaks for a particular congregation in a particular time and place; and it is not prayer, that is, it is not an honest attempt to speak to God but is, rather, a sort of sermonette with eyes closed, in which we make points to the congregation that we did not have the courage to make in the sermon, or we lecture God on current events and theological concepts.

My main point here is that free and liturgical prayer are not mutually exclusive. It is not that one form is "personal" while the other is "impersonal." They represent two ways of being with God. Liturgical prayer embodies the incarnational, institutional, historical, universal leading of the Spirit in our present prayer. These two forms of prayer complement one another when used with an awareness of their differing values.

GUIDELINES FOR PUBLIC PRAYER
(ESPECIALLY FOR PRACTITIONERS OF FREE PRAYER)

1. *Careful prior construction of a prayer does not mitigate against the concept of free prayer.* Isaac Watts, in his classic *Guide to Prayer* (1716), urged "conceived" rather than "extemporary" free prayer. A friend of mine speaks of the need for "premeditated" prayer, in which the pastor may compose a complete prayer in his or her study and then leave it there during the service. The experience of carefully thinking through the areas that one wishes to address in a prayer, working at the proper way to express these needs, and then letting this experience inform one's actual prayer on Sunday could be helpful. Other pastors may use a simple outline that they have formed after meditating on the lessons for that Sunday, on the sermon, on the season of the liturgical year, and on congregational concerns.

I once believed that young pastors should discipline themselves to write out their pastoral prayers until they gained sufficient expertise in public prayer and in the use of language. Lately I have come to see that this discipline is not a bad idea for seasoned pastors also. The longer we are in ministry, the greater the danger of our public speech slipping into "churchese" in which someone pushes our button and we start spewing forth pretty, religious-sounding words without the slightest thought behind them.

Prayer is too important for the church to do it without preparing for it. Preparation involves an active personal prayer life of your own plus the attempt to carefully construct your public prayers before you pray.

2. *Opportunities for congregational participation in public prayer should be explored.* One of the goals of worship leaders is to invite the people into the act. For instance, ask a few persons in the congregation to be prepared to offer one-sentence prayers of thanksgiving or petition at your direction. The old Anglican "bidding prayer"—in which the priest says something like, "Christian people, I bid you to pray for the needs of our nation; pray now for our country and its leaders . . . ," then a period of silence is observed during which the people may offer their own silent prayers—is a mix of liturgical and free prayer. It enables the pastor to guide the movement of the prayer while inviting the people to pray their own prayers for these needs. Or the pastor may use the litany form in which the people are told to pray some stereotyped response such as, "Lord, in your mercy, hear our prayer." The pastor then prays for various needs, ending each petition with a cue such as, "Therefore we now ask, Lord, in your mercy . . . ," after which the people respond, "Lord, in your mercy . . ."

If your congregation is small, you may receive spoken prayer requests before the prayers of intercession, or you may put cards in the pews on which parishioners may write specific concerns. These cards could then be dropped into the offering plate, collected by the ushers, and given to the pastor before the time for prayer. I know one congregation that posts a large sheet of paper with a pencil at the door into the sanctuary. As people enter, they may write concerns on this sheet. The sheet is then given to the pastor during the prelude, and the pastor can lift up these concerns in the pastoral prayer. The pastor might give people the opportunity to simply mention aloud the names of those who need prayer by saying something like, "O God, we now speak before you the names of those who need your love and care. . . ." Then the people spontaneously say aloud the first names of persons about whom they are concerned.

3. *A good service will have a mix of both types of prayer, free*

and liturgical, according to the movement of the service. For instance, we may open with a liturgical prayer of corporate confession, followed by a moment of silence for personal prayers of confession, ending with a prayer for forgiveness prayed by the pastor.

4. *Generally speaking, the trend in public worship is to include a variety of short prayers of various types rather than one long prayer that attempts to include everything.* The service may open with a short prayer related to the service of worship for this day. Then we may pray a short prayer for illumination before the Scripture is read and the sermon is preached. After the sermon, prayers for other people may be offered. Finally, a prayer of thanksgiving may be prayed when the offering is received and placed upon the table. These shorter, limited-focus prayers help the congregation to concentrate on one prayer activity at a time and to sense the variety of forms and purposes of prayer.

5. *A good pastor is a good listener.* The only justification for letting the pastor pray the pastoral prayer is that the pastor is the one who has listened to the congregation throughout the week so that the pastor may pray for the congregation on Sunday morning. The pastoral care thus becomes the preparation for prayer.

GUIDELINES FOR OUR LANGUAGE

Perhaps we ought to say a final word about the matter of liturgical speech. As we said, we pray through the language forms that are familiar to us and appropriate to the people of God. But lately, in our liturgical language, whether it be the language of prayers, hymns, sermons, or Scripture, we have been going through a crisis of language.

Much of the traditional liturgical language impresses people as stiff, dull, and overly formal. The modern world tends to be more casual and familiar. Many expressions and words no longer make sense. The archaic English of the Authorized Version of the Bible, the agrarian or monarchical metaphors of much of our biblical and liturgical speech, may be inappropriate or even incomprehensible to modern people. For instance, is it faithful and fair to speak of God by exclusively masculine metaphors: Lord, King, Shepherd, Father?

In an attempt to renew liturgical language, some of us have merely switched the older, archaic forms for superficial, banal, trivial speech. The latest slang expressions are not enduring or ennobling enough for our Sunday speech. Most of us would do well to immerse ourselves in one of the new worshipbooks of some of the denominations, such as the Anglican *Book of Common Prayer*, the Presbyterian *Book of Common Worship*, or the *Lutheran Book of Worship*. These are responsible attempts to renew our liturgical language through the use of good, formal, contemporary English. I have found, in the construction of my own free prayers for public worship, that I am helped by at least reading over similar public prayers in one of these books in order to help me with my phrasing and imagery.

As we construct our Sunday liturgies and speak in public worship, I suggest the following guidelines for our language:

1. *The language should articulate and enliven the Christian ideas that we understand to be essential to the faith.* Is it best to say, as does one of the prayers in the Communion service of the old *Book of Common Prayer*, that the faithful are "not worthy so much as to gather up the crumbs under thy Table"? Or in a more contemporary vein, is it theologically accurate to say that "God is a warm fuzzy to our souls"? Too many times we have traded allegedly archaic biblical metaphors for superficial pop-psychological or pop-philosophical ones. Our liturgical speech should attempt to be biblically based. It should draw upon the metaphors, symbols, and visions of the faith wherever possible. The Bible is a helpful guide for liturgical language, not only as a source of symbol and metaphor but as a guide in how to communicate the faith. Too often we preachers allow our public speech to become abstract, metaphysical, and vague. When the Bible talks about God, the Bible uses concrete, everyday images: the waiting father, the hen gathering her chicks, the lost sheep, the eagle's wings. Too often we speak of God through

big, abstract, high-sounding words—atonement, redemption, reconciliation, justification. We could learn from the Bible in this matter of religious speech.

2. *The language should not manipulate or call attention to itself.* Some contemporary attempts at language renewal are too "cute," too contemporary and faddish. "O God, smite us with our existence, slap us with reality, make us real, make us relational, we pray" was how I heard one pastor begin his prayer of intercession.

3. *The language employed should be an adequate idiom for this particular group and for this particular service.* There is a difference between appropriate liturgical language for a morning service on the beach during the youth retreat and the service of marriage in the sanctuary. There is a difference between the way we speak to four hundred people in a service of worship and the way we speak to fifty. It is not enough simply to make our speech "contemporary"; there are different kinds of contemporary English. The children playing on an elementary school playground, the longshoreman unloading freight at a dock, the judge handing down a judgment in a court of law are all speaking contemporary English. But they will speak very different forms of English, depending on the nature of the situation and what the language is supposed to be doing.

4. *Our language should be inclusive.* By now, we have rather conclusive evidence that when we use exclusively masculine pronouns in referring to God; when all our images of God are in terms of King, Father, and Lord; when all our references to people are in terms of men, mankind, and brotherhood; we are excluding the majority of our congregation through this linguistic sexism. When all our sermon illustrations concern the dilemmas of middle-aged businessmen, we are excluding the majority of our congregation. During worship we must be aware of the way our speech can exclude people on the basis of age, sex, race, and education. Obviously we want this divine-human encounter to be as inclusive as possible. While there may be areas of disagreement over what language is sexist and what is not, there is no disagreement that this is a pressing

concern for today's church and that attentiveness to our language can help our worship to include everyone.

Prayer, in public or in private, is speaking and listening to God. It is attentiveness of heart and mind to what God is doing and saying in our midst. It is the joyful, carefree task of being with the One who loves and is therefore loved; it is the difficult, deadly serious business of being attentive to the source of our life together. This is the activity toward which all other acts of worship are directed and from which all acts of service flow. Therefore, our leadership of prayer deserves our best efforts. I have come to feel that we should work as diligently at the construction, preparation, and delivery of our public prayers as we work at our sermons. Thus may the ancient prayer be ours today: "Let the words of my mouth and the meditation of my heart be acceptable in thy sight, O LORD, my rock and my redeemer" (Ps. 19:14).

4

The Table and the Font

Celebrating the Lord's Supper and Baptism

Actions speak louder than words. Words are fine, as far as they go. But sometimes the most important experiences of life are too deep for words.

God knows this. In the Bible, God not only says, "I love you," through the words of the prophets, the law, the sermons of Jesus, and the letters of Paul, but God's love is also demonstrated, made visible. "And this will be a sign for you: you will find a babe wrapped in swaddling cloths and lying in a manger" (Luke 2:12). This babe in the manger is a sign of the redemption of God's people.

We also see God's love demonstrated in symbols. Wedding rings, for instance, are powerful symbols that express, in a tangible way, the deepest and most inexpressible feelings of a man and woman. A flag, a handshake, a kiss, a cross, a wedding ring—these are symbols of love that say more than words can say.

"And the Word became flesh and dwelt among us, full of grace and truth; we have beheld his glory" (John 1:14). This text speaks of Jesus himself as the supreme, visible, and tangible symbol of God's love.

How fitting then, in a faith noted for its incarnality, its mundane, human qualities, that, when our Lord came to the end of his earthly ministry, he chose to show forth his truth through an intimate meal with loving friends in the upper room. Jesus thus gave his followers a sacrament, a symbol, a sign of love to share with the rest of the world. "Do this in remembrance of me," he said.

Then Jesus gave them a powerful sign of his redeeming, life-changing power let loose in the world after his resurrection. "Go therefore," he said, "and make disciples of all nations, baptizing them in the name of the Father and of the Son and of the Holy Spirit" (Matt. 28:19).

Sacraments and ordinances are everyday objects, like bread and water, and everyday actions, like eating and bathing, that when done among God's people in worship convey both God's love for them and their love for God. God uses everyday things we can understand—bread, wine, water—to show us a love that defies understanding.

THEOLOGY AND PRACTICE OF THE SACRAMENTS: ECUMENICAL AGREEMENT

How ironic, and how encouraging, that so many Christians who for so long felt separated at the Table and the font have, in recent years, discovered widespread ecumenical agreement concerning what ought to happen in the sacraments. The most striking feature of contemporary liturgical renewal is the emerging ecumenical consensus on baptism and the Lord's Supper. We shall identify some of the areas of theological agreement before discussing practical matters:

1. *There is widespread agreement on the biblical and historical centrality of baptism and the Lord's Supper.* We Protestants must admit that we have violated the biblical testimony on the centrality of these acts of worship by our infrequent and half-hearted celebration of the sacraments. As I said earlier, a full service of Word *and* Table is the normative Sunday morning

pattern for Christians. Also, baptism is a powerful sign of the nature of Christian life and the formation of the church. Recovery of robust, confident, frequent celebration of the sacraments is imperative.

2. *The theological focus of our sacraments has often been far too limited.* We have celebrated the Lord's Supper as a funereal, doleful memorial to a departed hero rather than the joyous Sunday resurrection meal it is intended to be. We have remembered only Maundy Thursday and the upper room and forgotten the meal at Emmaus on Sunday evening. This meal is a sign of the *presence* of Christ, not his absence. When we eat together, our focus is upon the whole saving work of God in Christ—birth, life, service, passion, death, resurrection, ascension, and present reign—not simply upon a reenactment of the somber meal in the upper room.

Likewise with baptism: in the Middle Ages, the theological focus of baptism became limited to human sin and cleansing from that sin. This approach overlooked the rich array of biblical baptismal images—death and life, power of the Spirit, refreshment, birth, renewal, ordination, adoption, circumcision, initiation, darkness to light.

3. *We have often made the sacraments into individualized, privatized acts of personal piety rather than the communal, familial, ecclesial acts they were meant to be.* Thus, the Lord's Supper was transformed into a quiet, introspective, individual meal with individual worshipers seeking salvation from individual sins—without communing with one another. Why would Jesus have chosen a *meal* with friends as a symbol of his kingdom if this were a private, lonely, individualized way of salvation? It is difficult to eat or to be saved alone. Every time that we celebrate the Lord's Supper should be an affirmation of our community in Christ and a means of forming the body around the Table.

Baptism is also a communal activity. Whenever baptism becomes a private gathering for the child's family alone, we have forgotten the necessity of the church in God's scheme of salvation. Baptism is often referred to in the New Testament as adoption or birth. Is it possible to be born by yourself—or to be born again by individual effort? You can't adopt yourself either. Baptism is a sign that Christianity is not a home correspondence course in salvation; it is a sign of a social, ecclesial, familial, gracious, communal way of life.

4. *The sacraments are linked to the most basic, primal, everyday experiences of life; to disjoint them from those human experiences is to undercut their power.* What do these sacraments mean? The Lord's Supper means everything that any meal means: love, fellowship, hunger, nourishment. These meanings are given added significance because, in this meal, we commune with the risen Christ, who joins us at the Table. People may not know what redemption, atonement, reconciliation, sanctification, and all our other big words mean— but everybody, from the youngest to the oldest, knows what a meal means. Therefore, when we celebrate this holy meal, our actions, elements, and words should make clear that this is a *meal*.

Baptism means everything that water means: cleansing, birth, power, refreshment, life, death. These natural, everyday meanings of water are given added power because this water is administered "in the name of Jesus." When we baptize, the congregation ought to see, hear, and feel *water*. Once again, some people may not know what justification, redemption, and prevenient grace mean—but everybody knows what it means to be thirsty, to be born, to drown, or to be dirty.

The Jewish faith has been called "symbiotic," meaning that it draws upon the experiences of everyday life for revelation. When we worship through wine, water, and bread, when we point to human events like a meal or a bath, we are linking our faith with daily life, spirit with flesh, the heavenly with the mundane. This linkage is essential for any relevant religion. Therefore we do a great injustice to the sacraments when we transform them into some ethereal, detached, "spiritual" exercise that has no support in everyday experience. Specifically when we celebrate these rites, we must use wine that tastes like wine and bread that looks and tastes like the bread we had for breakfast this morning. When we baptize, we must use water in sufficient amounts so that everyone sees, hears, and feels the experience of water.

We thus link our religion with our daily life. As Augustine once told his congregation: Every time the priest prays over the eucharistic bread on the Lord's Table, the priest is not saying that the bread on the altar is holy and the bread you had for breakfast this morning is unholy. The priest is focusing your attention, opening your eyes to the holiness of all bread, which comes as a gift of a loving God. So you taste the bread at Communion and say, "That tastes like the bread I had for breakfast this morning. Can that bread be holy too?"

Yes, the church says, precisely. You have gotten the point of our sacraments. Here are the signs of a God who is so close to us, so available to us, a God who continually, selflessly gives to us that we may be liberated and redeemed.

Now let me suggest some *practical implications* of these theological assertions:

1. *Restore the Lord's Supper to its rightful place in our Sunday worship.* Most of us Protestants need to do this. Quarterly celebrations are inadequate. In our worship life, infrequency usually breeds indifference and misunderstanding. Rather than making Communion "something special," as some churches claim to do, infrequent celebrations lead a congregation to regard Communion as something optional, unusual, and dispensable.

As the Reformers knew, Word and sacrament belong together. The Word must not only be preached, it must be practiced. In congregations where there has been long-term neglect of the sacraments, long-term reeducation may be needed. The best way to reeducate is through well-planned, enthusiastically led, frequent celebrations. Many of our people may not "understand" the Lord's Supper because they have never *seen* it. What they see, when they come to the Eucharist, is a stiff, cold, formal, make-believe meal with odd, make-believe food. Who can understand that?

Our church gives out a bread recipe to families in our

congregation. When the family bakes a loaf of bread and then presents that loaf on the altar on Sunday, everyone knows what Communion means.

I believe that the Eucharist should be celebrated at least monthly in a congregation. I like to celebrate it on the first Sunday of a new liturgical season, at Christmas and Easter, and on any other Sunday when the congregation wants to say, in effect: "This is a special time for our church. Today we want to do it up right, so we are having Communion." In celebrating the Lord's Supper in different liturgical seasons, we can choose hymns, prayers, and Scripture that will give a different focus to the meal, according to the season. This helps to overcome the complaint that, if we celebrate the Lord's Supper more often, it will become too familiar and lose its significance.

A wise pastor will try to fit the Eucharist into the pattern and style of Sunday worship of the congregation. One reason that people may resist the Eucharist is that it is done in an awkward, foreign style other than the worship style to which they are accustomed. If your congregation is not accustomed to reading the service from the back of the hymnal, do not insist that they do so on Communion Sundays. Simply go through the service, using the worshipbook yourself and having the people participate at your cues.

A pastor who served a rural area of West Virginia told me, "My congregation doesn't like to have Holy Communion." I said that that was impossible because (1) everyone not only likes to eat but also needs to eat and (2) all Christians want to be in the presence of Christ. I asked the pastor to tell me about his congregation. He told me that they were rural people with an average educational level of about eighth grade.

"That means you will not be able to use any printed material," I said. "Presenting them with long, written liturgies will only make them feel inadequate." We then discussed how the pastor might lead the service without having the congregation read the service from the hymnals.

While the pastor must respect the feelings and limitations of the congregation, there is no need to achieve unanimity of opinion before introducing new eucharistic practices. Sometimes people do not know what they like until they have experienced it over a period of time. I am confident that when we introduce eucharistic renewal with sensitivity—explaining what we are doing and why, and allowing the congregation opportunity for feedback and evaluation—the sacrament will speak for itself.

In the renewal that followed Vatican II in the Roman Catholic Church, Pope Paul VI spoke of "opening up the riches of the Church for the faithful." This reminds us that, in our renewal at baptism and the Lord's Supper, it is not a matter of introducing something new; it is a matter of uncovering the rightful heritage of the church in such a way that the people experience these riches anew.

2. *Utilize the new sacramental rites of your denomination.* Most of our older baptismal and eucharistic rites, which we inherited from the Reformation, are historically and biblically inadequate. They represent the Reformers' attempt to reform the worship of the Middle Ages, often through inadequate information on older practice. The new rites provide for much more congregational participation, stress the visual quality of the sacraments, lift up a wider array of biblical themes, and are constructed in a much more orderly, rational way. They use contemporary English without being faddish. Most congregations respond favorably to the use of these new resources.

3. *Preach and teach on the sacraments.* While the best way to renew the sacraments is simply to do them well, congregations appreciate some attempt to explain the meaning of these rites. For most Protestants, it is important to stress that the sacraments are thoroughly *biblical* experiences, not some "high church" vestige from the Middle Ages. The sacraments should be placed after the sermon in the Sunday order of worship. In this way we show that baptism is the fitting response to the good news and that baptism leads to full participation in the Lord's Table. Most Protestant congregations react unfavorably if their preacher appears to be emphasizing the Lord's Supper at the expense of a full sermon. While our preaching may be a bit

shorter on Communion Sundays, we should save our best sermons for these Sundays in order to underscore our belief in the linkage of Word and sacrament.

4. *Pay close attention to the mechanics of your leadership of these rites.* If the pastor appears to be ill at ease about his or her leadership of the sacraments, the congregation will feel that this rite is something strange and out of the ordinary. Carefully practice the movements and gestures that you will use in the service, preferably in front of a full-length mirror. Don't let a single action be missed by the people in the back row. The breaking of the loaf, the pouring of the wine, or the laying on of hands of the newly baptized should be seen by everyone.

In celebrating the sacraments, mechanics are everything. The main difference between a meal at a fast-food restaurant and a gourmet dinner is a difference in how the food is prepared and served. One system makes you feel like a cow being herded to the feed trough; another makes you feel like a human being. How do we make people feel at the Lord's Table by the way we serve them? No one should serve Communion who does not know how to hand someone a piece of bread in a gracious manner. No one should baptize a baby who is afraid to hold one. Our actions speak louder than our words.

Because the Lord's Supper is a meal, stand behind the Communion table, facing the people, like a host at a table. Use large, substantial vessels, preferably a single chalice and a large platter or tray. Begin the service with the table cleared, then, right before you give the prayer of thanksgiving, have the Communion vessels and the elements placed upon the table, as if you were preparing a meal. Likewise, after Communion, quickly clear the vessels and leftover food from the table. An appropriate amount of ceremony in preparing the meal helps to build a sense of expectancy in the congregation and also helps to link this rite with the meals they have known in daily life.

Because baptism is a sign of God's love and grace as well as a sign of inclusion into God's family, representatives from the congregation should assist you when you baptize someone.

Their presence helps to underscore the communal, corporate nature of this rite. When a child is to be baptized, have someone in the congregation (someone other than the child's parents) bring the child forward. The parents can follow as a sign that the whole congregation has responsibility for this child.

Sometimes, in the worship service when the Lord's Supper is celebrated, people complain that the service takes too long. If you are in a small congregation, this is usually not a problem. But where time is a factor, the length of the service is often more a matter of poorly planned and executed mechanics rather than a matter of too much substance. Have someone time the various acts of your Communion service. You may be surprised how time is used. Some pastors are shocked to find that they spend nearly as much time in announcements—reading the bulletin to the congregation—as they do in their sermon. My general feeling is that if time is a problem, do what is necessary to get the eucharistic service down to a manageable time frame.

Usually, the things that take the most time are the nonessentials rather than the essentials. What are the essentials for the Eucharist? First, the Word must be read and proclaimed. Then, after the prayers and the offering, you move to the Service of the Table. As Jesus gave the bread and the cup in the Communion, so do you. These are the essentials. Everything else is nonessential. If you have time for two anthems by the choir, fine. If you don't, you should eliminate them.

One of the most time-consuming aspects of many of the celebrations of Communion is the method of distribution. The elements should be distributed efficiently but in a manner that is not impersonal or rushed. The method of distribution may be a denominational and congregational tradition. Evaluate your method and ask if improvements can be made. Remember as you are evaluating that each method of receiving Communion—the people seated in the pews, kneeling at the chancel rail, standing before the altar—says something about what we believe is happening here. A congregation might want to try various methods of receiving Communion. Our congregation sometimes kneels for the distribution during the season of Lent and stands during the season of Easter, in order that our bodily posture may be attuned to the feeling of the season. The practice of dismissing each group of communicants that kneels at the Communion rail is repetitious, time-consuming, and without much liturgical sense. If your congregation kneels at the Communion rail, simply invite the people to come and go continuously. Ask them to hold out their hands when they are ready to receive the bread and wine; then, after they commune, they may continue to kneel in prayer or they may return to their seats at their own discretion.

During Communion, I like the old practice of singing hymns. This helps to lift the service and, by selecting hymns in accordance with the particular season of the year, we can focus the service in various ways. Sing hymns that are familiar, that the congregation can sing without looking at the hymnals, that are related to the particular season. This will do more to change the tone of your service than anything else. It also gives people something to do while the rest of the congregation is communing.

Avoid giving people detailed instructions on how to receive Communion. Too many instructions only make people uptight and make the service much more rigid and formal than it needs to be. A simple "Come to the Lord's Table" is usually enough. Visitors may be given brief instructions, or they can simply watch how the members do it. Generally speaking, ushers are unnecessary at Communion. Once again, ushers tend to make the service too formal and rigid with their stiff, lockstep directives. Most congregations, after they become accustomed to it, appreciate the freedom, the sense of unity, and the flow of a service in which they can move freely at their own discretion.

Likewise in our celebration of baptism, we must be attentive to the mechanics and the physical arrangements. The amount of water we use does make a difference. When we use a small finger bowl or an insignificant-looking font that is set off to the side of the sanctuary, we are saying something about the irrelevance of this rite. I use a large, crockery mixing bowl for baptism. Before the baptism, as the candidate is brought forward, a layperson presents a large pitcher of water for the baptism. Then, before the baptismal prayer, I pour the water into the bowl, making sure that the water is seen and heard. Baptism by immersion makes good biblical and symbolic sense, but pouring the water over the candidate's head, using a small bowl or baptismal shell, is also a satisfactory mode. Anything that can be done to lift up the visible, the audible, and the symbolic in our celebration of the sacraments is most helpful.

5. *Prepare people for more meaningful participation in the sacraments.* Every congregation should have an ongoing program of sacramental instruction. On a Sunday when the Lord's Supper is being celebrated, have the children's church school classes bake bread for the service. Your church might issue devotional materials that could be used around the family breakfast table on Communion Sundays before the family members come to church.

When there is a baptism of a baby, let the children visit the baby in the nursery before the service. Some churches let the children make small baptismal banners with the baby's Christian name, baptismal date, and a baptismal symbol on the banner. The banner is given to the baby's parents after baptism and is hung in the baby's room at home. A DVD of the service may also be given to the parents to play for the child at a future date, or a baptismal candle can be presented and then lighted on the anniversary of the child's baptism each year. The children's choir could learn a special baptismal song to sing to a newly baptized child to welcome him or her into the church. Since no person should be baptized without some instruction in the meaning and the responsibilities of this rite, I have a periodic class for parents who are seeking the baptism of their children. At this class we discuss the difficulties and joys of raising a child in the Christian faith. We explore the methods of family devotional practices, Bible reading in the home, children in Sunday worship, and the other skills and insights we need in order to bring this child into the faith. Whatever people's age at their baptism, we must be sure that we spend time educating them and their sponsors concerning this joyous mystery. All Christian education is part of the lifelong process of growing up into Christ, all part of living out the promises of our baptism.

This is one of the reasons that all baptized children in the congregation should participate in the Lord's Supper. Children learn by doing. A child learns how to eat by eating at the family dinner table. Young children grow by imitating their elders. It therefore makes good developmental sense to include the baptized children at the Table. As noted earlier, the sacraments are not merely a matter of understanding certain ideas in a rational way; the sacraments are symbols that are beyond our understanding. Children may not understand everything about the Lord's Supper, but they do understand this meal at a level appropriate to their stage of faith development. They know about the joy of meals, about sharing food and drink as a sign of love. They also know what it means to be included in—or excluded from—the family's special times.

We can think of no biblical or theological reason for the exclusion of children from the Lord's Table. If we baptize children, the reasons that would lead us to baptize the children of Christian parents would compel us to commune those same children. Our Lord has given children a special place in the kingdom. It would therefore be strange to have the family of God gathered on this most sacred occasion and then exclude these important members of the family.

Every time the water is poured and blessed in the Lord's name—every time the bread is lifted up, called holy, then broken and given in remembrance of him—the church enacts, in visible, tangible, human ways, the reality of his promise to us: "For where two or three are gathered in my name, there am I in the midst of them" (Matt. 18:20).

5

The Word in Worship
How to Construct a Biblical Sermon

In nearly every Protestant congregation of my acquaintance, preaching continues to be seen as the primary pastoral activity, the one from which all other pastoral leadership flows. We now turn to this central activity.

THE RENEWAL OF BIBLICAL PREACHING

The most exciting development in homiletics today is the renewal of biblical preaching. A number of factors contribute to this renewal:

1. While the primary purpose of the three-year Common Lectionary is to expose God's people to the reading of God's Word in a systematic, comprehensive way, *many pastors have found that the lectionary helps them to ensure that their preaching is also truly biblical.* Sometimes the lessons relate to one another, particularly the Gospel and the Old Testament; the Epistle usually goes its own way. Most of the time the pastor can preach on more than one of these texts only by doing an injustice to the message of each text.

The lectionary need not be a homiletical straitjacket. The preacher may deviate from the lectionary for good reasons: a local celebration, a civil holiday that the preacher deems appropriate for reflection in a sermon, some important event during the week. But, as a general rule, I try to discipline myself to stick with the lessons in the lectionary as the source for preaching. In so doing, I am forced to ponder many portions of God's Word that are unfamiliar to me or that challenge my pet theologies.

Some people say that by using the lectionary pastors forfeit their capacity for social activist, prophetic preaching. I have not found this to be true. In fact, I have much more opportunity to be truly prophetic because a congregation is more likely to accept the sermon's comments on controversial issues of the day if it is convinced that the thoughts arise out of the church's confrontation with its Scripture rather than out of the pastor's need to be relevant, judgmental, or abrasive.

2. Because the lectionary is now shared by many denominations, *there are more resources for the biblical preacher than have existed in the entire history of Christian preaching.* Many times pastors would like to employ careful methods of biblical interpretation in their sermon preparation, but this means digging through a stack of commentaries, detailed analysis, and hours of study—hours that many pastors do not feel they can spare.

Many clergy journals now give a synopsis of recent biblical interpretation of the lectionary readings for each Sunday. A wide array of books are available that offer more detailed study of the lections (as well as my own Pulpit Resource).*

Sermon subscription services that offer stock sermons based on the lectionary do more harm than good. Because they are prepared for a broad market, these stock sermons are usually too generalized, too popularized to be of great help to the parish pastor. Part of the beauty of your preaching is that it is

---

* Available from Logos Productions Inc., 6160 Carmen Avenue East, Inver Grove Heights, MN 55076-4422.

pastoral—a specific word addressed to a specific congregation by its pastor.

3. Finally, many preachers are showing a renewed interest in biblical preaching because they find, as the church has always found during important crises in its life, that *the Bible is the very source of our Christian identity.* We are living in a time when the church is having to expend more effort in defining itself, in nurturing its distinct identity, and in getting its values and its story right.

Many popular preachers of a generation ago specialized in "topical" preaching. The preacher would select a topic such as "How to Have Better Marriages" and then would string a group of interesting ideas together in a sermon. When the Bible was used in such sermons, the Scripture often functioned as a mere springboard for diving off into the pastor's opinions about the topic, or as a kind of religious tinting to the pastor's essentially secular ideas. To be fair to some of these topical preachers, many of them were so immersed in Scripture that they could imbue their topical preaching with biblical content.

Topical preaching can be helpful when the preacher addresses a topic that may not be a central concern of Scripture (e.g., nuclear power). There are also times when the sermon can best be constructed as a movement from some problem in contemporary life back to the witness of Scripture. Such topical or life-situation preaching should be done with great care, with the preacher honestly asking, Is the message of this sermon truly congruent with the witness of the church's Scripture and tradition?

On the other hand, proponents of topical preaching charge that exclusively biblical preachers sometimes run the risk of irrelevance, archaism, and dry, antiquarian detachment in their preaching if they assume that, simply by taking a biblical text and expounding it, they have preached a relevant word. As Harry Emerson Fosdick once commented, only a preacher could be so naive as to assume that the congregation is deeply interested in the fate of the Jebusites! Lectionary preaching and expository preaching (in which the preacher gives a detailed exposition of a biblical text) urge us to put the text in contemporary context; topical preaching urges us to let our present context inform our interpretation of the biblical text. These modes of preaching need not be mutually exclusive.

THE LECTIONARY AS A RESOURCE FOR BIBLICAL PREACHING: A METHOD

Here is one method for constructing biblical sermons. This is not the only way to go about it, but it is one that has been useful for me in moving from a biblical text to the sermon.

One helpful aspect of the lectionary is that it treats some biblical books sequentially—particularly the Synoptic Gospels and some of the Epistles. Thus, during Year A most of the year is spent with the Gospel of Matthew. You might begin your lectionary preaching by in-depth study of that Gospel since you will be preaching from it during the year.

1. First, *read the whole book through,* in one sitting if possible. Don't get bogged down in details. I keep a loose-leaf notebook, using a separate sheet of paper for each text. Take notes of first impressions. You will not want to lose these in a mass of later detailed study. At this point, don't worry about what you will preach; look for the forest rather than for individual trees. Get the "feel" of this book, the tone of it. Now you are ready to deal with specific texts.

If you use the lectionary as the basis for your Sunday sermon, you already have a text to work with—but not necessarily in the form in which you receive it. Sometimes the lectionary divides texts in ways that detract from the meaning of the text. For instance, the lectionary divides Luke's parable of the Prodigal Son into two Sundays; one Sunday deals with the prodigal's return, the next Sunday's text is the account of the older brother's reaction. Could you preach on either of these segments without referring to the parable as a whole? Where Paul begins a section of ethical exhortation, he often begins with "Therefore." In other words, what follows is based upon the preceding section. Can we do justice to Paul's ethical opinions without reference to the preceding theological precepts that give rise to the "therefore"?

First impressions are important. Note them well so they will not be lost amid later detailed study.

2. The next task is to *establish the text*. Whether or not you choose to use the lectionary as the source for your text, make sure that the text is divided logically. One of our homiletical sins is to take a word or a verse out of context and attempt to preach that rather than the text as a whole, for we can then fill the detached word or verse with our own opinions rather than listening to the whole message. I remember an uproarious mock sermon by the comic Flip Wilson, in which he took as his text, "There Shall Be a Sign." He then proceeded to preach a sermon on the theological meaning of various road signs! We abuse a text when we take it out of its context.

3. Now you are ready for *detailed word study of the text to make sure that you know what the text means*. Commentaries and lexicons are helpful here. Do you really know what the words mean in this context? For instance, the Gospel of John has a very different idea of the origin and work of the Holy Spirit than, say, the book of Acts. Jesus says, "Let the little children come to me," but do you know how ancient Near Eastern ideas about children differ from those of our day? The purpose of this study is to help us to be better listeners, hearing a text on its terms rather than through our preconceptions.

4. *Read the entire text again* with an ear toward its general thrust. What is the emotional bite of this text? Is it angry, sad, encouraging, judgmental, didactic? To whom was it first addressed? To whom might it be relevant today? Picture one individual in your congregation who needs to hear this text. What must happen in your sermon for that person to hear this text on its own terms? What experiences and dilemmas in that person's life relate to this text?

Many times, we lose the movement of the text under a mass

of details and dry, abstract ideas. In this final walk through the text, be attentive to the text as a whole.

Now is the time to begin making decisions about the sermon. I hope you have restrained yourself thus far and have resisted the temptation to spring from your first encounter with the text directly to a sermon. Many interpretive difficulties arise when the preacher jumps too quickly to the question "So what?" and seeks an instant sermon "payoff," an immediate relevance, from the text.

If you have waited to ask the "So what?" question, if you have restrained yourself, perhaps you have now "heard" a word in the text, perhaps a surprising word. What is that word? You can't preach on all your ideas about this text. What idea really grabs you, grabs you so much that you want to share it with others?

5. I still find helpful the time-honored practice of attempting to *state the theme of the proposed sermon in one sentence.* This sentence is the substance of my message. It will help me to control my sermon construction and keep extraneous elements to a minimum. The danger of this device is that it may encourage me to treat my text as an abstract, generalized idea that has been distilled from the text—such as "the real meaning behind the story of the prodigal son." I then preach an idea about the message rather than the story, which is the message. My congregation listens to ideas about a story rather than experiencing the story. In spite of this pitfall, I don't know where I'm going in writing the sermon until I can clearly state a theme.

6. Having determined, in one sentence, what I shall say, *how shall I say it?* Recently biblical criticism has urged us to be as attentive to the *form* as to the content and context. We therefore ask, "What was this language trying to say to its original listeners?" In order for the text to be heard today as it was heard at that time, we must attempt to use the same literary form. We will preach a poetic text differently from a historical account. If the text is a parable, then the sermon ought to retain that narrative quality.

Recently, the Epistle lection was a doxology out of one of the Pauline epistles. After looking at that text, I immediately began asking myself, "What is the idea contained in this text?" Then it occurred to me: The text is a hymn of praise. It means what it says—praise God! If the sermon is the result of boiling down this poetic text to some abstract idea, the sermon is not really preaching the text.

After this realization, I began to struggle with *how* to preach this particular passage. I decided to preach a doxological sermon in which I would simply refer to all the natural wonders and experiences of life that lead us to praise God.

After you have gone through these exegetical steps in which you have attempted to listen humbly and carefully to the text in its originating context, I advocate one more step before you begin to write. The first task of Christian preaching is to take the biblical text seriously. The second major task of Christian preaching is to take the congregational context with equal seriousness. As a pastor, you live in that congregational setting all the time. You are the essential link in the dialogue between the text and today's context.

7. Now listen to that congregational context and *jot down some ways in which your congregation needs to hear or can relate to this text.*

Does the text offer encouragement? Where does your church face discouragement? How can concepts like the second coming of Christ or the miracles or the resurrection relate to the needs of your people? How do your people differ from the first Christians to whom these words were addressed?

(If you are preaching topically, letting some contemporary concern rather than the biblical text be your starting point, you might move this last step to the very first. That is, listen to the contemporary context, then move to an appropriate and relevant biblical text and proceed with steps 2 through 6 as described above.)

Now you are ready to write, ready to use all the communicative gifts at your disposal to construct the sermon.

PITFALLS ON THE WAY FROM TEXT TO SERMON

As you exegete a given text and then interpret that text in your sermon, you are apt to encounter a number of common pitfalls along the way. As I said earlier, most of the trouble starts after the preacher reads the biblical text and asks, "So what?" In answering the "So what?" the preacher sometimes is tempted to draw meanings out of the text that are not justified by the original context or the plain sense of the text.

Here are some of the typical ways in which biblical texts are used (and abused) in sermons:

1. *Transference.* Scripture means today what it has always meant. Ascertain the plain meaning of a text, then adapt it to the situation. The disciples healed people; we can heal people. War is depicted in the Old Testament; war is permissible today. But transference, in its assumption that there are no differences between our time, our concepts, and our lives and those of the Bible, usually does injustice to Scripture. We read the Bible across a cultural and historical gap that must be understood and respected. The journey from what the text *meant* to what it now *means* can be a perilous one, requiring a knowledge both of the original context and of our situation today.

2. *Allegorization.* If a person believes that *every* portion of Scripture is useful for today's Christian, that person may be tempted to imbue troublesome or questionable passages with alleged symbolic meaning. The parable of the Pearl of Great Price will be anything that the preacher considers to be worth great sacrifice. Given sufficient imagination, allegorizers of Scripture can make the text mean anything they want, regardless of the plain meaning. As with direct transference, allegorization often ignores the historical context of the text.

3. *Parallelism.* The preacher draws a simple parallel between a biblical situation and a situation today. David's lie about adultery is a parallel to a contemporary president's lie about the federal budget and therefore deserves the same prophetic

rebuke or vice versa. Sexual immorality today is parallel to the sexual concerns of the prophets in the Old Testament. Admittedly, we are still human beings no less than were the people in the Bible. Yet, once again, parallelism takes our situation more seriously than the biblical context, ignoring historical and circumstantial dissimilarities in order to force a biblical text to suit our present questions and answers.

4. *Universalization.* A given text that applied to one situation is now applied to a whole array of circumstances. God delivered the Hebrews out of slavery, therefore God delivers all oppressed people. Jesus' admonition to "turn the other cheek" is applied to national defense. Universalization forgets that Scripture arises out of concrete needs of the community of faith in specific situations.

5. *Psychologizing.* A previous generation of preachers was often guilty of "spiritualizing" a text. The story of the manna for the wandering Hebrews of the exodus becomes an illustration of how, if people will trust God, they will receive spiritual sustenance. Today, a preacher is more likely to twist a text into some psychological truth. Joseph was thrown into a pit by his brothers; people today are often in the "pits" of depression. A man came to Jesus to be cured of his blindness; many today are "blind" to the beautiful world around us and to the needs of others. Close to allegorization, psychologizing arrogantly refuses to deal with the plain sense of the text and remodels the text to something more akin to twenty-first-century preoccupations.

6. *Moralizing.* Perhaps the most frequent modern interpretive pitfall is moralizing. This occurs when preachers attempt to draw simple moral inferences from the text, usually ideals that the listeners should practice or live. The gospel is presented as suggestions for better living, principles for correct opinion, or obligations to be met. The pastor, in an attempt to be relevant by presenting some straightforward plan of action for people to follow, turns every text into some simplistic, moralistic program.

The announcement "Blessed are the meek" becomes "How to practice meekness in everyday life." The story of the disciples being told to cast their nets on the other side of the boat becomes "If at first you don't succeed, try, try, again." The essentially God-centered concerns of Scripture are transformed into human-centered concerns. A parable about how God is like a father who waits for the prodigal's return becomes "How we may have better family life." Moralism unintentionally (but blasphemously) puts us in the place of God in Scripture, stresses people's misdeeds more than God's deeds, and talks about what we should do rather than what God is doing.

Few preachers are able to avoid all these pitfalls. In fact, any of them may be legitimate interpretive devices—*as long as we know that we are using a device that may abuse the meaning of the text if it is not employed with care.*

As we move in our study, from our conclusions of what the text *meant* back then to what it *means* today, we must approach the task with humility and with a healthy respect for the difficulties.

COMPOSING THE SERMON

Beyond these interpretive guidelines, I am reluctant to set down many other principles for building a sermon. Preaching is a learned skill; it is also an art. Should sermons have three points? Not necessarily. It depends on the text. Some sermons, as I said earlier, are best constructed as poems, some as a story or collection of stories. Others are straightforward exposition. It depends on the biblical text, the congregational context, the general message you are communicating, and your style as a preacher.

You might picture sermon construction as a series of blocks of material which, when combined, build a sermon. For instance, some sermons begin with the exposition of a biblical text, then move to the contemporary context:

> BIBLICAL TEXT
> (**What it says**)

> EXPOSITION OF THIS TEXT
> (What it meant)

> THE CONTEMPORARY SITUATION
> TO WHICH THIS TEXT SPEAKS
> (What it means)

Or you might let some contemporary issue illuminate a biblical text:

> CONTEMPORARY PROBLEM

> BIBLICAL TEXT THAT IS RELEVANT
> TO THIS PROBLEM

> WHAT WOULD HAPPEN IF THIS TEXT
> WERE APPLIED TO THIS PROBLEM?

When your biblical text is a story, perhaps it is best explicated through story:

> CONTEMPORARY STORY THAT PORTRAYS
> SOME ASPECT OF THE HUMAN CONDITION

> A BIBLICAL STORY THAT ILLUMINATES
> THIS SITUATION

Expend great care on the opening paragraph of a sermon. Here is where you will hook your listeners or lose them. Most preachers find that the more they preach, the simpler their sermons become. They learn to respect the limits of oral communication and how few ideas can be conveyed in one sermon. No sermon is complete until you have carefully gone over your manuscript or outline and deleted any superfluous or extraneous ideas, details, or illustrations that do not contribute to the development of the one-sentence theme that you defined at the beginning of the sermon construction process. Most congregations are appreciative when they can follow the logical development of a sermon and can take some specific idea or illustration home with them.

I prefer to write out my sermons in manuscript form. This discipline helps me to work on my phrasing, style, and content. However, I try not to take this manuscript into the pulpit with me for fear that I will be unduly tied to it, lose important eye contact with my listeners, and turn the sermon into a dry lecture.

In the pulpit itself, I speak from an outline that I made from the manuscript. By using an outline, I am confident that I know where I'm going, without being enslaved by my manuscript. I am thus free to spend more time underscoring some points my listeners do not seem to be understanding, yet still know that I will not wander aimlessly.

And so you rise to preach. The Word is read and then interpreted. When that is done, the Bible comes alive and thrives in its native habitat. In this manner the people of God are nourished and strengthened because you, their pastor, have listened to them and to the Word, with all the skills and gifts you have, and have dared to speak.

6

Giving the Word
Sermon Delivery

You have pored over your biblical text, using all your exegetical skills in order to listen to the text. Then, using all the hermeneutical skills at your disposal, you have constructed a sermon. Now we can come to the question of sermon delivery. Preaching is not the simple recitation of a manuscript. Preaching is an event, a visible, audible, communal moment that is a unique form of human communication. Sermon preparation and delivery is a conversational, dialogical affair; the pastor listens to the biblical text, asking questions of the text and allowing the text to speak, and then the pastor listens to the congregational context. Ultimately the pastor announces what he or she has heard.

Sometimes seminary courses in homiletics give students the impression that preaching is mostly a matter of composing proper ideas. Questions of correct doctrine, logical construction, and honest biblical interpretation are no small matters, as I said in the previous chapter. But in our concern with proper ideas, we preachers should be reminded that few laypersons listen to a sermon as a presentation of ideas. They know that in preaching, the medium is the message. The way a sermon is proclaimed is as important as are the ideas that the sermon attempts to communicate. It is difficult to draw sharp lines between the form of a sermon and its content, between style and substance, between the medium and the message.

Once I gave a group of laypersons a questionnaire after the service and asked them to answer a few simple questions about the content of the sermon. I was dismayed that they recalled very little of what I considered to be the message of the sermon. I was using "message" in too limited a way. The medium is the message. We must be as attentive to matters of style in a sermon as to matters of content. In fact, to a great extent *the style is the content.*

I can still remember, when I was a young child, listening to a preacher screaming at the congregation, pounding the pulpit, flailing his arms in the air, and shouting something about how much God loved us. The preacher was talking *about* love, but his style preached something else!

Effective delivery is perhaps the toughest aspect of good preaching. Delivery involves our personality, physical characteristics, native abilities, intellect, and a host of other factors. But be assured that effective sermon delivery can be learned. Delivery is not only a matter of talent, it is also a matter of training and practice.

GOOD PREACHING INVOLVES GOOD LISTENING

It takes two to preach: someone to speak and someone to hear. The aim of preaching is to enable better listening to the gospel. The test for preaching is never how eloquently we are speaking but how well people are listening. *Good speakers are always good listeners and keen observers.* So, in a sense, the first way to improve our preaching is to improve our listening.

Years ago I remember reading a book on public speaking that made one simple but very crucial point: there is only one rule for public speaking, "your listener's rule." Don't picture yourself before an appreciative audience of accepting and passive listeners. Sit where they sit. Think less about what you are saying in the speech and more about what they are saying to themselves as they listen. Where will they be bored, angered, uninterested, confused? Assume that they do not really want to be here today listening to you. Reach out to them, grab them, convince them that they really want to hear what you are saying. Good speakers are good listeners. How?

1. *Listen to the biblical text.* Much preaching today is boring and inconsequential for the simple reason that the preacher has nothing worthwhile to say—and knows it. When a messenger is truly engaged by an absorbing, important message, that messenger will find an appropriate way to communicate.

American preaching will be renewed when we are again attentive to the Word, when we are convinced that we have heard something unique to say. If you find nothing in Scripture that grabs you, it is doubtful that your sermon will grab someone else.

As was noted in the last chapter, listening to the text is not a matter of searching for some abstract idea that you can cut loose from the text and then preach. We listen for the movement of a text, the crisis point, the style, the emotional bite, as well as the ideas within the text. Listen as Jesus tells a story:

> "Every one then who hears these words of mine and does them will be like a wise man who built his house upon the rock; and the rain fell, and the floods came, and the winds blew and beat upon that house, but it did not fall, because it had been founded on the rock. And every one who hears these words of mine and does not do them will be like a foolish man who built his house upon the sand; and the rain fell, and the floods came, and the winds blew and beat against that house, and it fell; and great was the fall of it."
> (Matt. 7:24–27)

Read this story aloud. Note that it falls into two parts. The first half ends with the strong, clear word that the house stood "because it had been founded on the rock." The other half picks up tempo as the rain fell and the floods rose and the wind battered and beat the frail house until there was a great crash. *Slam! Bash!* And then silence. Jesus doesn't follow the story with a little moralism or labored explication. The story means what it says. First there is chaos: wind, rain, rushing flood; and then silence, the silence of judgment. The gavel has come down. One man's house stands, another's is swept away in chaos.

How would you preach this text so as to preserve the movement of the story itself? You might begin, as Jesus began, with an account of a person who formed her life on a sure foundation of sound values, firm faith, and enduring virtues. As Jesus says, the foundation consists of those who not only hear his words but also *do* them. You are not discussing just any foundation, but a foundation that consists of hearing and doing the will of God. Then the sermon could pick up tempo with an account of someone who assumed that all the rules were made for someone else and didn't apply to him—someone who haphazardly stumbled through life, assuming that it would all work out for the best somehow, someday. And then, alas, it all ended in a great crash. People live by their choices; they die by them too. They reap what they sow. When the floods come, then comes the judgment day. It is over.

Our first task is to bring people into contact with the text, confront them with it in a way that they hear it as though for the very first time. Jesus did not explain, explicate, or abstract this story. He simply told it, using all the narrative gifts he had, letting people hear it and respond to it in their own way. Any sermon on this text must go after the truth in the same manner.

If we do not carefully listen to the text, our preaching begins to suffer from boring sameness; all biblical truth is watered down to what sounds reasonable and practicable from our point of view. Therefore, our first listening task is to be ready to be surprised by what the text has to say, ready to listen and to dare to preach, no matter what.

2. *Listen to language.* This is a second principle of homiletical listening. Words are the tools of a preacher's trade. "A carpenter is only as good as his saw," a wise old craftsman once told me. Preachers must first be curious about the gospel; sec-

ond, they must be curious about speech. There are no effective preachers who are not fascinated by words. They enjoy varieties of speech, listen for rhythm in language, and relish picturesque verbal images.

Early in your ministry, develop the habit of reading frequently and widely. I read books on biblical interpretation and theology so that I will be a better listener to the gospel. But I read novels and biographies so that I will be a better listener to people and their lives.

I also find it helpful to listen to other preachers' sermons. I once participated in a small group of pastors who came together each week and listened to a taped sermon from one of the members of the group. Then the listeners responded to what they heard. This gave us feedback on our own preaching and also gave us the privilege of listening to someone else preach for a change. I also subscribe to a service that sends me monthly recordings of sermons. Many churches will mail their pastor's printed sermons for a small contribution.

Good preachers learn to listen to the work of other preachers and then to ask critical questions, such as: When did this sermon succeed and when did it fail? What about this sermon was especially appealing? How did the biblical text function in this sermon? What did the preacher's style of speaking do to the congregation? How does this preacher use language?

One reason that I compose my sermon in manuscript form is that the composing of the manuscript enables me to see sloppy language before I get into the pulpit and to strive for accuracy and vividness of speech.

Finally, a major problem for the preacher is the unfortunate tendency to use abstract, conceptual language rather than concrete, picturesque speech. Whenever we find ourselves talking with words that end in "-tion" and "-ism," we should be warned that our preaching may be slipping into "preacherese"—vague, abstract, platitudinous talk that makes religion sound like something out in never-never land. Use nouns and verbs more than adjectives and adverbs.

I have done an exercise with seminarians in a homiletics

class in which I had them list ten or twenty key concepts of the Christian faith, such as redemption, atonement, justification. Then I asked them to list one concrete noun from everyday, concrete human experience that embodies each theological concept. Don't preach about salvation; preach about being invited to a banquet. Don't preach about atonement; preach about being lost and found. This manner of speaking, keeping our speech closely linked to concrete human experience, provides an essential linking of the faith with everyday life.

3. *Listen to your listeners.* Most effective preachers do not need to be told when a sermon misses its mark. The eyes, posture, and restlessness of their congregation tell them all they need to know about a misfired sermon.

The primary reason that it is unwise to preach from a manuscript is that you may be tempted to read your sermon rather than listen to your congregation. Essential eye contact will be lost as you scan your notes. Carefully construct and practice your sermon so that you know exactly where you are going in order to be free to spend more time stressing those points the congregation appears not to hear or understand.

When you look at a congregation, really look at them, eye to eye. Look at their eyes, the expression on their faces, their posture. Pick out a couple of people for direct, intimate eye contact. Watch them before you rise to speak, and then watch them while you speak. They become a means of measuring how well your words are being received. Even in a large hall it helps to look at specific groups of people, to let them know that these words are not meant for all humanity in general but for them specifically.

Don't look at your listeners ceaselessly. Try staring at people, and you will find that they begin to look away. Look at your notes from time to time, or look away as you search for the right word or the next thought. Listeners like to see that you are thinking about your message, striving for the right word, and delivering a sermon that requires care and thought on your part.

Pay particular attention to the spoken words among the

people whom you serve. Particular styles of speaking give a community its distinctiveness, its identity. Whether for good or ill, we judge people by their style of conversation, their accent, inflection, vocabulary, pronunciation. Various ethnic groups are often noted for a distinct lingo that helps them feel a sense of unity, identity, and pride. Who are the people to whom you preach each Sunday? How do they talk?

A friend of mine was sent by her bishop to a small peach-farming community in South Carolina. She had lived only in urban environments. "I found that the everyday conversation of my people was virtually incomprehensible to me," she said. "I figured that if I had trouble understanding them, they could not understand me on Sunday. Therefore, I determined to spend more time with them during the week, listening to them, learning their distinct colloquialisms, mannerisms, and jargon."

4. *Listen to yourself.* "Know thyself" is a fundamental axiom for the preacher. What is your distinct speech personality? What do you look like when you are in the pulpit? Do you appear to be nervous, shy, and reticent, or do you come on too strong? Sometimes we send messages we don't intend to communicate. A friend of mine always prided himself on his relaxed, low-key, conversational style of preaching. He abandoned what he considered to be the pompous, bombastic oratory of older styles of preaching in favor of his more subdued approach. Yet when he had the opportunity to view himself on videotape, he realized that he was communicating sloppiness, tentativeness, and lack of conviction rather than relaxation.

This is a complex matter. Because our communication is a multifaceted affair, it helps to evaluate our preaching style both orally and visually, using the insights of others to help us. Don't worry about what you intended to convey by your preaching, worry about what your listeners heard.

A tape recorder can be helpful here. In one of my previous congregations, an individual taped every Sunday service on a cassette. At least once a month I sat down with the tape recorder, played back the whole service, and jotted down my impressions. I once noted that my voice seemed to be more animated and confident when I was preaching than when I was leading other acts of worship. My voice told me that I was more heavily invested in preaching than in other worship activities. I decided to spend more time preparing for my leadership of the prayers, creeds, and litanies.

The best means of evaluation is to use a DVD. Most preachers can locate someone who would record a Sunday service. Later, view the recorded sermon a couple of times so that you can overcome your initial shock at seeing yourself. Jot down your impressions. What do you need to do differently? Are you using any annoying mannerisms of speech or gesture? What about eye contact? Then view the sermon with one or two other people whom you trust so that you can compare your impressions with theirs.

In the more objective and relaxed climate of a few days after the sermon, you are freer to criticize—not to denigrate your work but to improve it, diagnose weaknesses, and prescribe corrections.

Visually, our goal is to communicate with our bodies in a manner appropriate to the words we are speaking. We can learn to control our body language. In a seminary counseling course we were taught simply to lean forward in the chair or to raise our eyebrows to indicate when we were particularly interested in what a counselee was saying. This nonverbal communication sent positive subconscious messages to the other person.

It is possible to choose our gestures, movements, and expressions as carefully as we choose our words. We do not want to lapse into unprincipled manipulation of the congregation or to draw attention to ourselves through corny, overly dramatic, contrived posturing. Pacing, rocking, wildly gesticulating, feigning tears, or wiping a fevered brow that is not really fevered does little to help us communicate sincerely.

Your voice, along with your body as a whole, is your primary instrument for communication in the pulpit. Not all of us are blessed with a resonant, stirring voice. But all of us can improve our voice. If, in your evaluation, you believe that you have a specific or major voice problem, get help from a trained speech professional. Some preachers spend their whole ministry being self-conscious and feeling inadequate because of their voice, when a few lessons from a speech therapist could help them.

While use of the voice is a complicated matter, far too complicated for in-depth treatment here, it may be helpful to note some frequent voice difficulties for you to ponder as you evaluate your sermon delivery.

Intensity. Some of us speak in ways that are understressed, dull, and subdued. Perhaps we believe that the weight of our thought alone is enough to carry the sermon. Sometimes we have become overly dependent upon a sound amplification system. Because we have not listened to our own voice, we do not hear how dull we are.

Try this exercise. Choose some passage from the Bible—for instance, the parable of the House Built on the Rock. Read it into a cassette recorder. Now take the same passage and record it by consciously "overdoing" it; ham it up, dramatize the words with as much intensity as you can. Now play back both readings. Which one would you rather hear? Which one does a better job of enlivening the text? Probably you will find that you like the second, more intense reading better. We usually overestimate our vocal intensity, thinking that we are sounding more articulate than we do. As you move from a tape recorder to a large auditorium, your intensity has to increase proportionately. The larger the architectural space, the more dramatic and emphatic should be the inflection and articulation of your voice.

Many women ministers report that their congregations complain about the lack of intensity in their voices. In part, this is due to people's stereotyped images of what preaching ought to sound like. Many women have voices that are softer, less intense than men's voices. At times, this will be a virtue—when a soft voice is called for. But in the pulpit many women find that they must intentionally use their voices carefully, not stridently but firmly and boldly, so that their preaching will be heard.

Vocal intensity also depends upon the use of your whole

body. Good singers sing with their whole being. Posture is important: feet squarely planted a comfortable space apart, muscles toned but not tight, shoulders up and slightly forward. An adequate supply of air is needed, so always speak from the diaphragm, letting your lower abdominal muscles control your lungs to take in air swiftly and let it out slowly. When we are nervous, our vocal muscles contract and the muscle action moves from the diaphragm to the neck, which results in a higher pitch and a nervous, breathless quality to the voice. Take a moment before you begin to speak to consciously relax your muscles by breathing in deeply and slowly letting the air out, relaxing your throat and voice in the process.

Intensity should be correlated to what you are saying. Be slow and deliberate when you are laying your groundwork; pick up tempo and volume when you are moving to a climax. Most of us need to speak much, much slower. It takes time for the sound of your voice to travel out to your listeners, for their minds to sort the auditory images they are receiving, and for them to think about what you say. Nervousness makes us talk too fast. Intensity of voice therefore does not mean talking louder and faster; in fact, intensity tends to build when we take our time and make sure that every word is heard and savored by our listeners.

Clarity. Many times our listeners miss what we say because we have not clearly articulated the vowels, diphthongs, and consonants in our words. Clarity of articulation arises from clarity of thought. Stumbling, slurred articulation occurs when we have not been as careful about our manner of expression as about the thoughts of what we are expressing. Once again, it helps to slow everything down. Never hesitate to pause when your listeners need more time to collect their thoughts about what they have heard. Well-placed moments of silence help to give words more impact. Are you moving your mouth when you speak? Check your facial expression. Does it fit what you are trying to say? Generally speaking, it is difficult to overdo the articulation of mouth, tongue, and jaw when you speak. Such careful physical movement is the source of verbal clarity.

Variety. Many of us speak as if we were a one-note song or a record player with its needle stuck in the same groove. Inflection is the change of pitch. Many preachers develop the habit of always lowering their inflection on the syllables at the end of phrases:

> Jesus
>   said,
>   Come
>   unto
>   me,
> all ye . . . that are
> heavy
>   laden.

This delivery is tiresome. Movement of pitch up and down, related to the words we are saying, helps to give diversity to our speaking. It suggests a complexity to what we are saying, whereas a monotone pattern suggests boredom, sameness, and drabness.

Vocal variety also involves your distinct personality. One reason your preaching is interesting is that you are interesting; you are different, distinctive. In seminary I confessed to my preaching professor that I was very self-conscious about my southern accent and my rather high voice. My professor gave me tapes of sermons by some of the twentieth century's great preachers: Harry Emerson Fosdick, Halford Luccock, Clovis Chappell, Henry Sloane Coffin. When I listened to the tapes, I found that all these preachers had distinct regionalisms in their speech. Nearly all had rather weak, high voices, and most displayed some speech habit or impediment. But they were all fascinating. They all had turned their "handicap" into an advantage. Luccock, for instance, had a habit of ending a paragraph by trailing off into a little high-pitched note. It became his speech trademark and kept grabbing your attention to what he was saying.

How dull if all preachers' voices sounded like the bland, nondistinct, flattened-out speech of the television news commentator. Let the Word come through who you are and the way you speak, and let your distinctiveness be an aid to your listeners rather than an annoying obstacle.

PRACTICE MAKES PERFECT

The better prepared you are, the more relaxed you will be. We are best able to spontaneously adapt ourselves to the state of the congregation and to the people's needs when we have prepared in the most detailed fashion.

I have established the habit of practicing my sermons, at least their beginnings and endings, in my sanctuary early on Sunday morning or late on Saturday afternoon. It helps me to hear the sermon in its native habitat, to listen for the sound of the words, to imagine my congregation present, to feel myself moving within the flow of the sermon. Some preachers record their sermons and play it back later, making notes on their manuscript or outline as they listen.

Because I am now more aware of the importance of body language in preaching, I deliver part or all of my sermon in the middle of the chancel area rather than solely behind the pulpit. The pulpit boxes me in, shields me from my listeners. I may read the Scripture and begin the sermon behind the pulpit, then move naturally out into the chancel area as the sermon progresses, ending the sermon as I move down nearly to where the first row of pews begins. This pattern may not seem natural for every preacher, but it works for me, and I can tell that my congregation listens more expectantly and intently when I move from behind the pulpit. This style of preaching requires me to more than double my practice for delivery. Once again, the more relaxed and spontaneous a preacher appears, probably the more he or she has carefully practiced for the sermon.

In that moment when the congregation settles itself in the pews, that moment after the sacred text has been read and all is quiet and expectant, the people look to you. You are the preacher, the essential link between them and the good news.

Without you, the good news is not news; no one hears or believes. Call it a burden, call it a privilege, or a duty; you know that it is worthy of your best talents, worthy of a lifetime of labor and dedication. On any Sunday you can give it all you have and still know that the Word deserves more. It is no small task that the church has set upon your shoulders.

So as you enter the pulpit to offer the Word, pray to God for the gifts needed for the task, for the persistence and energy to develop those gifts, and for the courage to use them to God's glory and for the edification of the church. Being called to preach the gospel, you can do no more than to promise, as long as you have breath and as long as there is someone to listen, by God's grace, that you will give them the Word.

7

Text and Context
Sermon Planning and Evaluation

Good sermons need time to grow. When do you begin sermon preparation? You are always engaged in sermon preparation as you go about your duties, because the pastor does not cease being a preacher when he or she begins a pastoral counseling session or chats with a parishioner at the corner grocery. You are doing the essential listening that will provide you with the questions, issues, insights, images, illustrations, and answers that make your preaching relevant, engaging, and truly biblical.

In this chapter the focus is on the skills and insights whereby we grow in our ability as preachers by gathering and using appropriate homiletical materials and by evaluating our sermons.

USING, ABUSING, AND COLLECTING ILLUSTRATIONS

Laypersons often complain that their preacher's sermons are not down to earth, not understandable, and not interesting. What they mean, more than likely, is that their preacher is not proficient in the use of illustrative material. An illustration does just that: it illustrates or illuminates a topic. Sermons that are completely narrative in nature or poetic preachers whose speech is colorful and concrete need no further use of illustrative material. But most of us, in most of our sermons, need stories, mental images, poems, words, and phrases that make our speech vivid and illuminating to everyday human experience. Therefore, a major ongoing task for the preacher is the collection and appropriate use of sermon illustrations.

Illustrations have fulfilled their purpose when our listeners say, "That's it, that's how it is in my life. I see." We do not use illustrations as mere stylistic ornamentation. A pointless joke, told at the beginning of a sermon, completely detached from the rest of the sermon, is an affront to an intelligent congregation and to the gravity of the gospel itself. Strings of entertaining but unrelated stories only confirm the congregation's hunch that the preacher has nothing to say—and knows it—and therefore attempts to hide the sermon's emptiness with a batch of cute anecdotes.

Other preachers may use illustrations to intimidate the congregation with a contrived display of their reading or erudition. Some pastors give the congregation lectures on Greek verbs, ancient history, or their latest trip to the Holy Land or recent chat with the chief justice of the Supreme Court. The illustration calls attention to itself, blocks understanding rather than illuminating the message, and degenerates into a spurious attempt to preach themselves rather than Jesus Christ as Lord.

The main requirement for the inclusion of an illustration is the simple, utilitarian test: *Does this help to illustrate and illuminate the biblically derived point I am trying to make?*

All of us remember a story in a sermon long after we have forgotten the abstract concepts. Use stories with care. A story of particular intensity, making a peculiarly strong point, can overwhelm everything else in a sermon. (Perhaps you should consider telling only that intense story and letting it be the sermon.) By all means, use it late in the sermon, perhaps at the very end, since everything else you say after the story will be anticlimactic.

Generally speaking, illustrations should be short; if not, the congregation may bog down in an overly involved story or a string of anecdotes. If you need to give half the plot of the movie in order to use an illustration from one scene, don't bother. The sermon's movement will be interrupted, and the congregation will have long since lost interest and forgotten the point you were trying to make. For the same reason, illustrations should not be placed back to back. Place them carefully throughout the sermon to give emphasis and bite where you need it. On the whole, most sermons need more illustrations rather than fewer, particularly the sermons of inexperienced preachers. When a preacher realizes that the sermon is running a little long, he or she usually lops off a couple of illustrations instead of retaining the illustrative material and cutting out the number of ideas being covered. Most sermons should deal with only a couple of ideas that are well illustrated from life experiences.

If you need to explain an illustration for it to make sense, don't use it. Personalize your illustrations when you can. Put them in your own words. Give credit where credit is due, but avoid tedious quoting from other sources. However, you must get your facts right. Be careful not to make glib references to complicated psychological or economic data. There may be a number of persons in your congregation who know more about those subjects than you and will be annoyed by your amateurish reference to their disciplines without taking the trouble to get the facts. Sometimes preachers are tempted to embroider the truth a bit or to report some incident that happened to someone else as if it had happened to them. Such dishonesty never rings true with the congregation and finally undercuts the proclamation.

Keep illustrations varied and inclusive. The preacher who is a football enthusiast must avoid a football story in every sermon. If all your illustrations concern the dilemmas of a middle-aged businessman, you have thereby excluded the larger part of your congregation. Don't forget the variety within your congregation when searching for appropriate illustrations: not everyone may have been to college; some are young or unemployed or unmarried or childless. The point of an illustration is to include listeners and to illuminate the Scripture.

Since the purpose of an illustration is to enable the gospel to hit home where people live, anything from the world of human interest can be a potential illustration: newspapers, television, magazine advertisements, everyday conversation, current events, family life. These become a mirror to our lives, give specificity and contemporaneity to our preaching, and put the text in our context.

But people also appreciate having their world expanded by the pastor. Literature, art, science, and industry offer an inexhaustible supply of metaphors and images for the sermon. A friend of mine talked me into accompanying him to a wrestling match. The whole thing impressed me as a needless waste of time—a celebration of violence at worst, bad theater at best. Later, as I was struggling with the Easter text from Colossians, which proclaims that Christ "disarmed the principalities, triumphing over them, making a spectacle of them," I remembered the wrestling. I thought of this mock warfare between "good" in the white trunks and "bad" in the dark velour trunks. I saw wrestling in terms of a drama between the forces of righteousness and the forces of darkness in which good always wins—and I had an illustration for the triumph of good over evil on Easter.

"Nothing bad ever happens to a writer," was how an author once put it. Everything is potential grist for the preacher's mill.

Needless to say, the Bible is a vast resource of illustrative material. Awhile back I was reflecting on the then much-discussed midlife crisis that adult developmentalists were documenting. I was making a point about how we sometimes get lost on life's journey at its midpoint and can't find our way. I knew lots of examples among my own congregation, but I certainly did not want to use these people as illustrations. Then I remembered the story of David and Bathsheba in 2 Samuel and realized that midlife crisis is nothing new. David became my illustration of the dynamics of a contemporary malady.

Poetry is particularly problematic as illustrative material. It is rarely helpful to quote more than a couple of lines of poetry in a sermon. Many good poems are difficult to understand at first hearing. Bad poetry may be easier to understand, but it often trivializes the gospel and weakens a sermon through cheap sentimentality. The same limitations apply to the use of poetic material from hymns. I find particularly tiresome the practice of ending every sermon with a quote from some hymn.

Occasionally, we may use illustrative material from our own experience, but there are dangers here. Congregations quickly tire of stories about how cute the pastor's children were last week or the spiritual trials and tribulations of Pastor X. The only reason for using personal illustrations is to link our message with everyone's life.

In the use of personal illustrations there are a few guidelines. First, we must be careful not to use an illustration that might embarrass someone or that might divulge some pastoral confidence. "A woman said to me the other day during a counseling session . . ." is an illustration sure to reduce greatly the pastor's counseling load.

Second, a good test for personal material is the question, Could this experience have happened to anyone in the congregation? If this event could only have happened to a Baptist pastor on the third floor of General Hospital, it should be avoided. We do well to ask ourselves, when we use personal material, Who is the "hero" of this story? We should probably be the antihero, the Everyman in our stories about ourselves rather than the spiritual virtuoso or the moral Superman. Let us not forget who is supposed to be the real hero of our preaching.

Don't bother with books of sermon illustrations. Most of the material there is already overused, out of date, and too generalized to be of much value. More important, it is not yours. Such illustrations will obviously have been lifted from somewhere and set into the sermon. The congregation knows that you are not an expert on Broadway plays, popular music, Roman history, or the number of hot dogs consumed each day in New York City. There is no substitute for a personal, believable meeting of the preacher with the Word.

Not that it is unhelpful to read other sermons. The value of other people's homiletical work is not as a source of imitation or a field for gleaning bits and pieces of potentially useful illustrative material, but rather as examples of how other preachers build upon their own experiences, reading, and reflection to make the Word live for their listeners. The beauty of preaching is that all-too-rare moment when your congregation realizes that it is hearing the testimony of someone who has been there, standing before the Word, wrestling with the Word in his or her own life and experience and then daring to share that with others.

I find it helpful to use my pocket computer for jotting down images, ideas, stories, bits of conversation, and other potentially illustrative material. Do not rely on memory for this material. When recording an illustration, record in detail. Rather than writing "People in shopping mall," which will probably mean nothing to you six months from now, write your detailed impressions:

> People walking, constantly walking, eyes glazed at the neon lights and the shouting advertisements. Buy this. Try us. Look here. Walking but not buying. Too many choices. Drifting without direction. Life is choices but sometimes there are too many choices, so we are numbed by it all, wander to nowhere, drift.

By recording your illustrations in detail, you retain the immediate, specific, concrete power of the moment, which helps illustrations to breathe and live again when used in sermons.

The careful collecting and filing of sermon illustrations is a skill that makes effective preaching possible. A friend of mine is a wildlife artist who carves birds out of wood. His garage is filled with odd pieces of lumber, all picked up at random and carefully saved for that day when one of them may be just what he needs to finish a project. Of course, for my friend, and for me as a preacher, the trick is to store this necessary building material in such a way that it can be found when needed. There is the problem. Any system of filing illustrations is better than no system. Some preachers have elaborate computer search systems. Others use loose-leaf notebooks. Some simply drop clippings and notes into a big box, which they paw through every so often.

I use two systems. Because I preach from the three-year lectionary, I know which texts will be appearing on any given Sunday in the cycle. I therefore make a file folder for each Scripture passage for every Sunday in the year. Whenever I happen upon an illustration or exegetical insight which relates to that passage, I clip or copy it and drop it in the proper folder. Then, when that Sunday rolls around, I already have material which has been accumulating on that passage. When I finally construct a sermon on the passage, I file that sermon in the same folder when I am finished.

Every year or so, it is good to spend an afternoon sorting through your material for anything that has become out of date. The point of illustration is to give the preached word immediacy and relevance, so antiquated illustrations have less value. Also, if you save everything, your file will eventually become utterly unmanageable.

There is a danger in becoming too enamored of the process of discovering and retaining sermon illustrations. The danger is that we might let the illustrations become more important than our engagement with the biblical text or the congregational context and begin building sermons around particularly appealing illustrations. Once again, the function of illustrations is to *link the biblical text with the congregational context.*

EVALUATING YOUR SERMONS

Unfortunately, the last opportunity for sermon criticism most of us had was in a seminary homiletics class. Since then, we have changed, our listeners have changed, and the goals of our preaching may have changed. Are our listeners really hearing us?

As I noted in the last chapter, your listeners are constantly communicating with you as you preach—everything from the vacant stare, to the "Nice sermon today, preacher," to the "You made me so angry this morning." Do we hear what they are telling us about our preaching, or do we only hear what we want and filter out the rest?

Sometimes we cannot use lay feedback in our preaching because it is in a form that is difficult to use. What does a preacher learn from the "Nice sermon today, preacher"?

When someone in the congregation strenuously objected to your sermon last week, is that a sign of homiletical failure or success? Is lay approval the sole test of good preaching? Of course not. I have said that preaching must be evaluated first by biblical criteria: Was this sermon faithful to the scriptural text?

But in order to be faithful to the text and to the purposes of the Bible itself, the sermon must speak to and be heard within today's congregational context. We must attempt for the sermon to be heard by contemporary listeners the same way that the text was heard by the original listeners. Biblical preachers care about congregational reaction to preaching *because* they are biblical preachers.

When I was young, I preached a sermon on a text from Jeremiah. Typical of that prophet's words, the text was a harsh, straightforward denunciation of the religious laxity of Jeremiah's day. Consequently, my sermon also had a hard edge to it.

To my dismay, a parishioner responded by saying, on her way out the door, "At first I was upset by what you were saying, but then I looked at you, and thought how sweet you were, and knew that you didn't really mean what you were saying."

I was saying one thing, but she was hearing something else. Was my sermon faithful to the biblical text? Not unless my words were congruent with the purpose, results, and function of the biblical Word.

In the previous chapter I mentioned the value of asking fellow pastors to evaluate your preaching, which can be a helpful means of growth since other pastors may provide informed peer criticism of your work. A few guidelines for peer criticism: Any process of peer criticism should be reciprocal. Ask evaluation only from someone who is willing to let you evaluate his or her sermons. This helps to remove some of the threat and temptations inherent in peer evaluation. Agree to evaluation of more than one sermon in order to get a fair picture of your style. Preferably, video should be used; however, evaluators can listen to an audiotape. The weakness of peer evaluation is that fellow clergy are not your congregation. They may have the same clerical prejudices and values that cause problems for your congregational listeners when you preach.

Therefore, there is no substitute for devising some means of eliciting accurate, usable congregational response to your preaching. This is not easy. There is a halo effect around the pastor that makes people reluctant to let the pastor know that they are critical. Negative evaluation of the pastor also reflects negatively on their church. Many laypeople simply suppress their honest opinion about their pastor's preaching.

People's initial response to a sermon will probably be positive. As time passes, and the people find that their pastor is serious about obtaining their criticism, negative evaluation will come.

A METHOD OF OBTAINING
LAY RESPONSE TO SERMONS

One pastor whom I know met with an adult church school class at 9:45 each Sunday morning and led the group in a study of the lections for that day. She then shared what she intended to preach that day and how she had constructed her sermon. After the morning service, she met with the group for thirty minutes of feedback.

I prefer to use the more formal technique of a short questionnaire, which gives me more specific and detailed feedback than I may be able to obtain in an informal discussion. The questionnaire I use was designed by Dr. Boyd Stokes, who studied the factors that make up a "good sermon" by questioning congregations, pastors, and professors of homiletics. The complete questionnaire is found in the appendix.

Every year or so, I randomly select twenty members of the congregation and ask them to attend every Sunday for a five-week period and complete this questionnaire at the end of each service. The questionnaire can be completed in a few minutes, yet it covers a wide array of homiletical qualities. The results can be quickly tabulated so that they can be quantified and compared.

When tabulating, note that items 3, 5, 7, 8, 9, 10, 13, 19, 20, 21, and 23 are negatively stated so that the score in these items needs to be reversed in order that all scores will be comparable. (Half the questions are stated negatively to discourage respondents from haphazardly answering all questions in the same way.) Thus, a score of 5 on item number 3 would be reversed to 1, and so on. The lower the total score, the more favorable the respondents are to your preaching.

You may wish to focus on particular aspects of your preaching, say on your eye contact, which is measured by item 10. Intentionally try to look at your notes less often and then see if your respondents feel that you have improved this problem from one sermon to the next. Ask respondents to put their birth date in the upper right corner so that you will be able to compare individual sets of questionnaires.

My score actually went down in some areas as the evaluation process continued over a period of weeks. My respondents had become more astute listeners. This is one of the fringe benefits of asking laypersons to evaluate sermons. The laypersons gain sympathy with difficulties involved in proclamation and a renewed respect for their preacher who trusted them. Few of us enjoy hearing criticism of what we do, particularly when we are doing something as spiritually, emotionally, and intellectually demanding as preaching, and yet, because communication of the gospel is a dialogue between the biblical text and the congregational context, we must make sermon evaluation a major part of our personal growth as preachers.

8

Getting Everyone into the Act
Lay Involvement in Planning
and Evaluating Worship

You may be asking yourself, How can I make this happen in
my congregation?

Your enthusiasm, commitment, and competency as a
preacher and leader of worship are the first keys to the renewal
of worship in the church. Enabling you to be that sort of pastor has been the chief purpose of this book.

The next key to making it happen in your congregation is
the formation, training, and use of appropriate worship committees and task forces that involve members of the congregation in planning, evaluating, and leading worship.

Why involve the laity? Many people tend to think of the
Sunday service as the sole domain of the pastor. This thinking
must change. It is theologically indefensible to see the Sunday
assembly as the last area of exclusive clerical prerogative. The
principle of the priesthood of believers affirms that it is the *people* who are the "priests" to the world by virtue of their baptism.

The pastor is the enabler, teacher, servant, and priest of
these priestly ones. A clericalized, sacerdotal presbyterate, in
which a clerical upper crust lords it over the lowly laity, is an
ecclesiastical deformity. Liturgical leadership that prays,

praises, witnesses, sings, interprets, responds, and offers *for* the faithful or *in place of* the faithful is a sign that the church has yet to believe the gospel Word that "You are a chosen race, a royal priesthood, a holy nation, God's own people, that you may declare the wonderful deeds of him who called you out of darkness into his marvelous light. Once you were no people but now you are God's people" (1 Pet. 2:9–10).

Liturgical renewal is church renewal. You have already noted, in our discussion of the Lord's Supper and baptism, for instance, the new stress on these signs as acts of the community. We are talking about a family at the dinner table, a family adopting a new child. This communal, social, corporate way of salvation must be evident, not only in our rites themselves but also in our planning and leadership of those rites. Therefore, lay involvement is essential.

The laity may need some encouragement before they join in the act of worship preparation. They have had many, many years of exclusion in these matters. But, generally speaking, we clergy are the ones who need to be coaxed to invite them into the act. It may be difficult for us to let go. After all, worship is one of the last exclusive clerical domains. Sometimes, a pastor who is deeply committed to "quality" liturgies, which are well stated, carefully executed, and fully formed, may not be willing to risk turning things over to the laity. Besides, a pastor is a busy person. It is quicker and easier simply to do it yourself, impose it upon them, and hope that it suits them rather than to risk the educating, training, arguing, and persuading that lay worship involvement requires of the pastor. It may be quicker and easier, but whether, in the long run, such one-sided leadership is either effective or faithful to the purpose of the church is another matter.

This call for lay involvement in no way denies the necessary function of the ordained ministry. Good pastoral leadership does not stifle the priest within us; rather, it calls forth and encourages our shared priesthood. Poor leaders botch everyone else's ministry. The function of worship leaders is to allow the faithful to exercise their own God-given ministries of praise, offering, witness, and intercession. Good pastoral leadership strives to get everyone into the act.

THE WORSHIP AND MUSIC COMMITTEE

Committees that enable lay involvement in worship planning and leadership may be organized in any number of ways. Your denomination may have its own model.

I suggest a standing Worship and Music Committee. (Larger parishes may need two separate committees for these two functions.) The Worship and Music Committee assists the pastor in:

1. Ensuring that the services are conducted in accordance with the rites of the particular denomination.
2. Recruiting and training acolytes, lectors, altar guild members, and ushers.
3. Ensuring the care of paraments, vestments, and liturgical utensils.
4. Supporting the musicians of the church and ensuring that the choir has the music supplies and instruments that it needs to lead congregational music.
5. Assisting the pastor in planning and evaluating, and at times leading the congregation's worship.

A decade ago there may have been little need for this committee. In our period of liturgical change, this could be one of the most active committees in your church. Select your most creative parishioners for this committee, particularly those who are adventuresome as well as sensitive to your congregational traditions and opinions. They should be people who are willing to learn, to risk, to listen, and actively to seek congregational response to liturgical innovation.

A number of groups will be under the care and supervision of the Worship and Music Committee:

Acolytes not only provide assistance to the movement of the service but also enable younger members of the congregation to learn about and participate in worship. Generally, very young children, while they may look cute, should not be used as acolytes. Many churches form an acolyte club, which inducts and trains new members and provides fellowship and recognition for acolytes. Well-trained acolytes, who are made to feel like important pastoral assistants in the service, are a significant aid to good celebration.

Lectors have been discussed in an earlier chapter. The Worship Committee must establish some method of choosing and training people for the essential task of reading Scripture.

Altar guild members are appointed to care for the worship area and its furnishings. They must be people who are convinced that the community's worship deserves an attractive, neat setting with the brass polished and the linen clean and pressed.

Ushers must be recruited on the basis of their ability to set a comfortable, hospitable climate in the worship area. Every church needs a head usher who invites people who have the necessary gifts, appoints assistants as needed, and continually trains and evaluates the appearance, duties, and role of the ushers.

The Worship and Music Committee may find it helpful to appoint other specialized subcommittees such as a wedding committee, which aids in the preparation for, direction of, and cleanup after weddings in the parish. A funeral committee could fulfill the same duties for parish funerals.

WORSHIP TASK FORCES

The Worship and Music Committee will have its hands full ensuring the week-to-week oversight of the congregation's liturgical needs. Laypersons can take an even more active role in the planning and leadership of specific Sunday services through the formation of a worship task force, which is convened for the purpose of working with the pastor on particular services.

The task force is formed by the Worship and Music Committee to focus upon some specific project. Because my church realized that many of the newer members did not have a background of frequent participation in the Lord's Supper, we formed a task force that studied interpretive materials on the sacraments with the pastor, conducted a survey to uncover congregational questions and confusion about the sacrament, and then composed a booklet on the Lord's Supper that is now given to new members.

Because we became increasingly concerned about the place of children in our worship, we formed a task force that collected information on what others are doing in this area, sponsored two speakers on the subject, and eventually presented a list of recommendations to our Worship and Music Committee and our Christian Education Committee.

The Worship and Music Committee also decided to form a couple of task forces a year to work with the pastor on enriching the worship during a particular liturgical season. Some pastors may be willing to spend the time required to involve the laity in planning every Sunday service. Most of us, however, find that we do well to pick a couple of periods during the year, of a few weeks' duration, in which we actively try to engage a small group of laity in planning the services for that period.

For instance, early in September, you might work with the Worship and Music Committee to convene a small group of persons to plan the services during Advent. In the first session you tell the group what its task is: to study the lessons for Advent; to review and evaluate what the congregation has done in the past during this season; to explore possibilities for innovation in the ritual, visual aids, music, and proclamation during Advent; to construct services for this period; and to plan supporting educational experiences. Your role in the task force is that of teacher, coordinator, and adviser. You also have the final say in what shall be included in the Sunday services that the task force plans. With one person acting as coordinator and evaluator, it is hoped that unity and coherence of the service will be maintained. However, you must convey a genuine willingness to risk experimentation, to trust the gifts of the group, and to honor—within the limits of theological integrity, historical values, and pastoral responsibilities—the wishes of the task force.

The task force needs to know what Advent is. What are the goals of the church in this season? What is an appropriate focus for your Advent Sunday celebrations? Take the people through a quick overview of the lectionary readings for the period. Have them discuss what images, ideas, themes, and feelings are suggested by these texts. Then review what your church has done in past Advents, perhaps examining copies of past worship bulletins with them. Ask them to study the lessons carefully before the next session.

At the second session of the Advent task force, take each service from the First Sunday in Advent to Christmas Day and list them on separate sheets of newsprint. Ask the people to help you decide which lesson or lessons should determine the focus of each service. List a central image or theme for that service.

Once you have established the overall theme for each service, begin planning the detailed order of worship. Go through the pattern for worship (chapter 2) and discuss how you will do each activity. For instance, how shall you gather? Last Advent, our church decided to work on the theme "Light in the Darkness." People entered a darkened sanctuary in which only a few lights were burning. No flowers were used in Advent. Only the Advent wreath was near the altar. We hoped that the physical setting would suggest a subdued, somber tone. The service began with someone standing up before the congregation and reading a newspaper story or some recent clipping that illustrated our "darkness": statistics on the arms race, a story of an impoverished refugee family, or something else that was a contemporary reminder of the darker side of life. This was followed by a moment of silence.

Then, from the rear of the sanctuary, a reader spoke scriptural words of expectancy and hope. (The appointed Old Testament lessons from Isaiah or the Epistle usually fit nicely.)

Then the clergy, other readers, and choir processed in as all stood and sang, "Come, Thou Long-expected Jesus" (or "O Come, O Come, Emmanuel," or some other Advent hymn).

In each part of the Sunday pattern, the task force tried to ask how we could do the acts of worship in ways that were congruent with the texts for the day. We solicited litanies and prayers from selected church school classes. We asked a couple in our church to sew a banner that depicted the "Light in the Darkness" theme. Children's church school classes were asked to design bulletin covers to illustrate each Sunday's focus. The Christian Education Committee planned an intergenerational gathering on the First Sunday in Advent in which families and individuals made their own Advent wreaths to use at home along with an Advent devotional booklet written by members of the young adult fellowship.

Those who are responsible for music should be present at every meeting of the task force so that the music can be coordinated with the other liturgy. We devoted at least fifteen or twenty minutes of each session to brainstorming on images, ideas, and questions raised by the lections or the sermon for that day. I collected these comments and read them later in composing my sermon. The whole process of study, collection, and planning required a total of four two-hour meetings.

Because of the work of the Advent task force, our services had a richness and variety that I alone could never have given them. Time and again, the congregation was visibly moved by the offering of some individual or group who had composed and led some act of worship.

One of the main values of an experience like the Advent task force is educational in nature. Those laypersons who composed the task force gained a new understanding of and appreciation for the worship of the church. I daresay none of them will ever glance over the Sunday order of worship without some deep sense of what has gone into the planning of that service. I could foresee a pastor conducting an extensive program of liturgical education simply by convening two or three task forces a year, each composed of different parishioners who come together to work on worship. Note that the task force not only plans and leads the service itself, but also searches for ways to educate and involve the rest of the congregation in the act.

EDUCATION FOR WORSHIP

Liturgical education is a continuing concern for the pastor. If you work through the Worship and Music Committee and its seasonal task forces, you will always have a core of people in your congregation who are informed, experienced, and committed to continual liturgical renewal.

New members need to be oriented in the liturgical practices of your congregation. Perhaps an experienced member of the Worship and Music Committee could serve as an instructor for new members before they join your church.

Children's church school classes should be seen, in part, as a means of preparing children for more meaningful participation in congregational worship. Every child should be taught such liturgical materials as the Lord's Prayer, the creeds, and the frequently used choral responses. Before a baptism or a celebration of the Lord's Supper, the pastor might meet with the children and discuss their questions about the sacraments. Every now and then the pastor could take a moment in the Sunday service to call the children forward to explain to them some act of worship in terms that they can understand. Many adults themselves will undoubtedly welcome these explanations!

Sermons that refer to baptism, the offering, the prayers of intercession, or other acts of worship help to link the act of preaching with other parts of the liturgy. From time to time, you might even preach a whole sermon on some liturgical activity—though we must restrain our Protestant compulsion to explain and to rationalize everything and to treat the liturgy in a didactic fashion.

If your church uses a printed Sunday bulletin, periodic notes on various acts of worship or proposed changes are a possibility. Most people welcome any pastoral attempt to enable them to participate more meaningfully in worship. As noted earlier, the primary reason liturgical innovation fails in a congregation is that no one took the trouble to explain to people why this change was being made.

Ultimately, liturgical education comes through doing rather than through teaching. As noted in our earlier discussion of sacramental renewal, the best way to engage the laity in worship is for us pastors to lead the celebration with competence and conviction. If you lead the people of God in worship with enthusiasm and expectancy, they will follow in kind. If you don't, all the classes, seminars, and explanations in the world will not move them.

So, whether you are preaching or praying, whether you are leading the faithful in praise or following them in offering, let all you do be done to the greater glorification and enjoyment of God. Thereby may the Word be unleashed, the people of God be fed, the priest be faithful to the call, and the God who saves be pleased.

CONTEMPORARY OR TRADITIONAL?
REFEREEING IN THE "WORSHIP WARS"

In recent years many congregations have been exploring "contemporary" worship. New forms of prayer and new acts of worship are being utilized with mixed results. Most of the tension in most congregations relates to experiments in music. Praise bands, electronically produced and recorded music, and small singing ensembles have replaced the traditional choir with organ and piano. Rock, bluegrass, New Age, and jazz styles have pushed out the more staid harmonies of Bach, Wesley, and Watts. Tensions between "contemporary" and "traditional" worship have led some to speak of our period as the time of the "Worship Wars" as pastors, musicians, and people choose up sides and battle over which worship is truly faithful Christian worship. Most pastors today must therefore have the ability to lead the congregation in sorting out the conflicting claims of opposing sides in the debate and refereeing amid the competing claims. In any pastoral situation, it is not enough for a new pastor simply to ask, "What are you accustomed to doing on Sunday morning?" Responsible pastors must fulfill the role of teachers, consultants, evaluators, and resource persons for the changing worship life of any vibrant congregation.

So-called traditionalists tend to see the so-called contemporary advocates as dangerously discarding the church's treasured liturgical riches, disposing of time-honored sacred music, and replacing it with superficial tunes that are more suited to be used as jingles in radio advertising than for the song of the body of Christ. For their part, some of the "contemporary" crowd see the upholders of tradition as hopelessly mired in the "we-never-did-it-that-way-before" defense, unconcerned about the church's need to evangelize a new generation of young Christians, and succumbing to boring and irrelevant worship practices without trusting the Holy Spirit to lead us in new directions of praise.

Neither of these positions is very helpful. More helpful is to stick to the question with which we opened this book: *Will our rituals enable the church to do what it needs to do when it gathers to worship?* I have found it helpful, in the heat of the "Worship Wars" in my congregation, to remember a few guiding affirmations:

1. *Worship is one way that the church participates in the "communion of the saints,"* a main means by which we join our prayer and praise with that of the saints who have preceded us in the faith. Worship therefore tends to be one of the most "traditional" acts in the church's life. Thank God that we are not left to our own devices, not forced to reinvent the wheel as far as our conversation with God is concerned. We are not the first to walk the path of faith. The saints can show us the way. The church's rich tradition guides us. One of our responsibilities is to nurture and to form new Christians, introducing them to the practices of the faith that others before them found helpful and necessary. More than changing the worship to suit the limitations of the people, we ought to change the people to enable

them faithfully and richly to worship. Just as you must submit
to learning a host of "traditional" words, rituals, and rules if
you are to learn to play the sport of baseball, so also you must
submit to a large amount of tradition if you are going to learn
to pray as a Christian. Rather than dumb down the worship of
the church so that anyone wandering in off the street can "get
it," we ought to do a better job of preparing people to exuber-
antly join in the church's praise, welcoming newcomers with,
"Here is the way we worship. We love it, and we want to help
you love it as well."

2. On the other hand, *the worship of the church has always
been in a process of growth and development.* We serve a living
Lord, not a dead antique. The Holy Spirit is active in all sorts
of artistic forms, musical styles, and diverse expressions of
faith. Much of our worship is too limited to the present culture
of that congregation. Part of the fun of being a Christian is
being part of the church universal. Faithful Christian worship
is always, to some degree, multicultural and multilingual. Any
time a congregation gathers and finds that it is limited to the
tastes and inclinations of one generation, one gender, one language, one culture, that congregation ought to push itself to
explore more of the richness of the Christian past and present
in prayer. A prayer from the sixteenth-century German Reformation, a song from contemporary Zimbabwe, a Bach cantata,
all in response to a sermon from a Minnesota preacher is a service that comes close to approaching some of the richness of the
Christian faith. The future of Christian worship is not so much
"traditional" or "contemporary" but rather *eclectic.*

3. *Whenever the church gathers, we are engaged in a mutual
sharing of diverse gifts.* All Christians know the delight of praying a prayer, or singing a song that is new and unfamiliar—that
means something to someone else in the church, but not to
us—only to discover that, in the praying or the singing, the
song becomes meaningful to us as well. A new dimension has
been added to our spiritual life. We are enriched in the innovation. Christians therefore ought to be pushed to develop a
sense of openness, a willingness to risk trying out something

new and different, as well as to practice patience in allowing our fellow Christians to enjoy various forms of prayer and praise that, at least at first hearing, mean little to us. Few people respond positively to, "You mean you don't know this hymn? Everyone else does!" Rather, "Here is a new hymn that really fits with today's gospel lesson. We would like to share it with you now," is a gracious invitation to spiritual growth. The test for any act of worship may not be so much, "Do I personally like this song or not?" but rather, "Is my neighbor who sits next to me in the pew enabled to worship God in this act of worship or not?"

4. *The issue is rarely a simple matter of "traditional versus contemporary" but more typically a matter of familiar versus unfamiliar in worship.* Today's contemporary service becomes, in just a few months, tomorrow's rather predictable, boring routine. There are many Christians today for whom a two-hundred-year-old hymn by Charles Wesley would be an uncomfortably innovative experience. A good service ought to have a mix of the comfortably familiar and the uncomfortably risky and experimental. A good service gives us a safe, comfortable sense of knowing where we are and who we are in this time of worship but at the same time a sense of exploration and spiritual venture. Too much predictability in worship, and boredom is often the result. Too much risk accompanied by the anxiety over what is going to happen next, and we are overwhelmed.

5. It never ought to be a question of "Should we try something new or not?" The question again is, *"How can we be more faithful in our worship?"* The first question is not, "Would our people enjoy singing this hymn?" but rather the questions raised should be: "Is this hymn a valid expression of our faith? Is it biblical? Does it employ theologically sound images? Is the style of music appropriate to what the people of God want to sing and say in this service?" While we have stressed the desirability of the pastor utilizing lay leadership in planning and leading worship, the pastor must never abdicate responsibility as the chief evaluator and teacher of worship.

The pastor is responsible for asking of any act of worship, whether that act is familiar or unfamiliar: "Does this represent, at least to a high degree, the richness and the depth of our faith in Christ?"

6. When it comes down to it, in evaluating worship, particularly music for worship, it is not so much a matter of "traditional versus contemporary" but rather a question of *quality.* "Give of your best to the Master," we used to sing in church youth group. It's still a good guide for worship planning and evaluation. The worship of the church deserves our best efforts. Sometimes "traditional" worship impresses us as dull and boring because it is poorly planned and unenthusiastically led. Bach done poorly is bad Bach. Sometimes "contemporary" worship impresses us as superficial, banal, sentimental, and sappy, because it is poorly planned and unenthusiastically led. Some music should not be played in a Christian church because there is no one there to play that type of music well. A traditional hymn played conscientiously on a piano is far better than the very best of contemporary "praise music" butchered by a band of people who, while perhaps sincere and well intentioned, have clearly not been called by God to lead in Christian worship!

It is enough for most people simply to relax and enjoy Sunday worship as the praise of God. The Westminster Shorter Catechism even defines our purpose as human beings as nothing more purposeful than the delightful "to glorify God, and to enjoy [God] forever." That's worship at its best.

However, for someone who is a pastor, a person who is called from among the baptized to lead God's people in prayer and praise, one of your responsibilities is critically to evaluate and examine worship in order to enable this experience to be all that it can be for God's people. While you may be so busy, on most Sundays, leading the service that you have little time or inclination to evaluate and critique the service, spend some time either alone or with your Worship Committee, and take a critical look at the service as a whole.

The pastor, in leading and evaluating worship, is fulfilling much the same pastoral responsibility as when the pastor preaches—holding God's people up to the standards of God's word in Scripture, enabling Scripture and tradition to call forth the church as it is meant by God to be. Thomas G. Long, after studying the worship of a group of vibrant churches, found the following characteristics in their congregational life and worship.* These churches:

1. Make room, somewhere in worship, for the experience of mystery.
2. Are very intentional about showing hospitality to the stranger.
3. Have recovered and made visible the sense of drama inherent in Christian worship.
4. Emphasize congregational music that is both excellent and eclectic in style and genre.
5. Creatively adapt the space and environment of worship.
6. Have a strong connection between worship and local mission, a connection that is expressed in every aspect of the worship service.
7. Have a relatively stable order of service and a significant repertoire of worship elements and responses that the congregation knows by heart.
8. Move to a joyous festival experience toward the end of the worship service.
9. Have strong, charismatic pastors and worship leaders.

How does the service at your church measure up to these criteria? And how do you as a worship leader appear to the congregation when you are leading? Perhaps there was a time in the church when, in most congregations, "good worship" meant simply opening up the service books and following the service just as it was followed last Sunday, and the Sunday before that

---

* Thomas G. Long, *Beyond the Worship Wars: Building Vital and Faithful Worship* (Washington, DC: The Alban Institute, 2001), 30–31.

as well. Our day is different. It is our calling to be part of that generation of Christians who must rethink our worship, must seek fresh forms of prayer and praise, confident that God will give us the gifts we need to worship God faithfully in thought, word, and deed.

To be honest, all worship is "contemporary." That is, all Christian worship is an experience of God here and God now. The God who once seemed distant or unavailable to us graciously comes close to us. We have that mysterious but undeniable experience of the living, personal, active God—Father, Son, and Holy Spirit. All of this is a gift of a God who, in love, is here, now. Ultimately, engaging worship is a gift of this living God, not the result of our anxious efforts. We come seeking God only to be delighted to discover that God is seeking us. We are busy saying something to God only to be surprised that God is speaking to us. That's true worship.

God's presence among us is not to be summoned forth through our hard work at worship leadership (even by reading good books on worship leadership!). One of the things that makes the worship of the church so wonderful is that "good worship" is an undeserved gift of a God who graciously comes and goes among us, the uncontrolled presence, the movement of the Holy Spirit. Still, though we cannot hope to predict or to control the coming and going of the living God, we can take heart that the God of Israel and the church tend to bless our earnest efforts to be faithful servants, in our words and deeds of worship. Our careful planning and honest evaluation of our prayer and praise is one means God uses to bless our times of worship.

On the Sunday after Easter, the lectionary has us read this portrait of life in the post-Easter church:

> Now the company of those who believed were of one heart and soul, and no one said that any of the things which he possessed was his own, but they had everything in common. And with great power the apostles gave their testimony to the resurrection of the Lord Jesus, and great grace was

upon them all. There was not a needy person among them, for as many as were possessors of lands or houses sold them, and brought the proceeds of what was sold and laid it at the apostles' feet; and distribution was made to each as any had need.

(Acts 4:32–35)

This is the church's strongest visible evidence of the truth of our resurrection faith—a resurrected community in which everything has been made new through our worship. Strangers who once had little in common have become sisters and brothers at the Table of the Lord, praising God with a unified voice. Old, deadly economic and social arrangements have been overturned. Here is truly "testimony to the resurrection" in this transformed people, transformed by a power that has descended upon them from on high. Here is the world re-created as God meant it to be, where "there was not a needy person among them" and all things are seen as gifts entrusted to us by God rather than possessions to be tightly grasped.

Every Sunday, when we receive the offering, when gifts of time, talent, and money are placed upon the altar, this act of worship is meant to be a grand summit toward which all of our acts of worship move us. The church, having heard the Word, now embodies the Word, enacts the Word, moving from worship to the world. The Sunday offering is meant to be a revolutionary, countercultural, and prophetic act for the church. There are few more inflammatory and potentially disruptive acts than when the pastor stands and announces to the congregation that it is now time for the offering. Here embodied before the congregation on Sunday is what the pastor ought to be doing all week—inviting us to give God what is rightly God's, to show that our money is where our hearts are (Matt. 6:21), and to feel the needs of someone other than ourselves.

When our well-formed worship produces transformed lives, when the words we speak to one another and to God in worship become the work we perform for God and one another in the world, that is Sunday as it is meant to be, that is worship in "spirit and truth" (John 4:23), that is God's great gift. God with us. At last, God will get that which God desires.

And God will finally have what belongs to God.

> *"See, the home of God is among mortals.*
> *He will dwell with them as their God;*
> *they will be his peoples,*
> *and God himself will be with them. . . ."*
> (Rev. 21:3)

Appendix

Sermon Reaction Questionnaire

Please do not sign your name. Please supply the following information:

A. SEX (1) male ____; (2) female____

B. AGE (1) up through 19 years ____; (2) 20–29 ____; (3) 30–39 ____
    (4) 40–49 ____; (5) 50-59 ____; (6) above 59 ____.

Please indicate whether you agree or disagree with the following reactions to the sermon you have just heard. This includes both the content and the delivery of the sermon. Indicate your reactions on the scale as follows:

Circle 1 for Strongly Agree, 2 for Agree, 3 for Uncertain, 4 for Disagree, 5 for Strongly Disagree

Your honesty and frankness will be appreciated.

1. 1 2 3 4 5 maintained my interest
2. 1 2 3 4 5 integrated the sermon into the total service of worship
3. 1 2 3 4 5 did not inspire me
4. 1 2 3 4 5 involved his or her personality in the message
5. 1 2 3 4 5 did not both deal with and illumine the Scripture chosen as the text
6. 1 2 3 4 5 used words and thought patterns in present-day usage
7. 1 2 3 4 5 did not evidence a personal confession of faith
8. 1 2 3 4 5 lasted too long
9. 1 2 3 4 5 was not very well understood by me

10. 1 2 3 4 5 looked at or read his or her notes too often
11. 1 2 3 4 5 projected an attitude of love for us
12. 1 2 3 4 5 spoke to some of my personal needs
13. 1 2 3 4 5 did not sufficiently emphasize the greatness of Christ
14. 1 2 3 4 5 was made more meaningful by the reading of the Scripture
15. 1 2 3 4 5 showed self-confidence
16. 1 2 3 4 5 was more readily accepted by me because of my previous feelings for the minister
17. 1 2 3 4 5 was made more meaningful by the appearance of the worship setting
18. 1 2 3 4 5 made me feel a oneness with him or her
19. 1 2 3 4 5 seemed to speak down to us
20. 1 2 3 4 5 did not have a sufficiently forceful conclusion
21. 1 2 3 4 5 did not initiate an encounter between God and myself
22. 1 2 3 4 5 contained points that were easy to remember
23. 1 2 3 4 5 did not make me eager to serve God any more than I have served God up until now
24. 1 2 3 4 5 led me to accept the message

Index